Good Housekeeping

The Complete Clutter Solution

Good Housekeeping

The Complete Clutter Solution

Organize Your Home for Good

C. J. Petersen

Hearst Books
A Division of Sterling Publishing Co., Inc.
New York

Every effort has been made to ensure that all the information in this book is accurate. However, due to differing conditions, tools, and individual skills, the publisher cannot be responsible for any injuries, losses, and/or other damages that may result from the use of the information in this book.

Good Housekeeping

Ellen Levine	Editor in Chief
Richard Eisenberg	Special Projects Director
Marilu Lopez	Design Director

PROJECT EDITOR: SUSAN RANDOL
BOOK DESIGN BY ELIZABETH VAN ITALIE

Library of Congress Cataloging-in-Publication Data
Peterson, Chris, 1961-
 Good housekeeping the complete clutter solution : organize your home for good / Chris Peterson.
   p. cm.
 Includes index.
 ISBN 1-58816-453-5
 1. Home economics. 2. Housekeeping. I. Title: Complete clutter solution. II. Good housekeeping. III. Title.
 TX147.P39 2005
 640—dc22
                    2004026525

10 9 8 7 6 5 4 3 2 1

Published by Hearst Books
A Division of Sterling Publishing Co., Inc.
387 Park Avenue South, New York, NY 10016

Good Housekeeping is a trademark owned by Hearst Magazines Property, Inc., in USA, and Hearst Communications, Inc., in Canada. Hearst Books is a trademark owned by Hearst Communications, Inc.

www.goodhousekeeping.com

For information about custom editions, special sales, premium and corporate purchases, please contact Sterling Special Sales Department at 800-805-5489 or specialsales@sterlingpub.com.

Distributed in Canada by Sterling Publishing
c/o Canadian Manda Group, 165 Dufferin Street
Toronto, Ontario, Canada M6K 3H6

Distributed in Australia by Capricorn Link (Australia) Pty. Ltd.
P.O. Box 704, Windsor, NSW 2756 Australia

Manufactured in China

ISBN 1-58816-453-5

Contents

Foreword

This book is for anyone who has spent 20 minutes looking for the remote, moved homework to put dinner on the table, searched high and low for that favorite sweater only to find it crumpled under a stack of dirty clothes, or missed paying a bill on time because it was stuffed in a junk drawer. If this sounds even a little bit like you, take heart. You are not alone. Almost everyone has to deal with a disorganized home to one degree or another.

This doesn't mean you're messy or a bad person. It's just that life is more hectic than ever. As we become busier and busier, our homes become more disorganized and clutter seems to take over. Fighting the battle against clutter is exhausting. We can straighten the whole house and clean top to bottom, but within a week the chaos is back. What's the answer? Develop solutions that win the war against clutter and banish messes forever.

At *Good Housekeeping*, we've created a system to do just that. By dividing each room into manageable zones and devoting less than an hour a day, you can get your home completely organized—in less than a month. After you've made the clutter-beating changes that are right for your home and your family, you'll have to spend no more than a few minutes each day to keep clutter from creeping back in. We've even included a "Keeping Up" section at the end of each chapter to help you stop clutter from coming back.

This complete plan for organizing the home is simple, logical, and realistic. We give you strategies for attacking each zone, and advice on how to reorganize the area and eliminate the clutter. Even if you don't have the time or energy to organize the whole room at once, you can probably find time to get it done zone by zone. At the beginning of each zone we have included a clock icon to give you an idea of how much time you need to set aside to complete that zone. The system is simple: The shading on each clock tells you how long each zone will take—roughly 15 minutes, 30 minutes, or 1 hour. This system lets you plan when to tackle a zone based on how much time you have. There's nothing worse than getting halfway through reorganizing a closet only to find that you have to run to pick up the kids, get to work, or do an errand.

The Complete Clutter Solution is not about "straightening up." It's not about how to clean better or faster. It's about making real changes that will alter the way you use the space in your home so that you don't create clutter in the first place. The fixes can be as simple as hanging a hook for your keys so you never misplace them, or as complex as outfitting your drawers with organizers so that everyone in the house knows exactly where things belong.

The Complete Clutter Solution will help you avoid frustration. The task of organizing each zone is broken down into manageable chunks, so you never feel overwhelmed. We've also included helpful tips and insights. You'll find regular boxes called Dollar Smart that will help you save money and realize good value in anything you buy to help you organize. Storage in Style boxes provide simple and quick ways to make your home look great with new organizational aids. And keep your eye out for the Inside Scoop boxes—they give you ingenious, little-known facts and strategies that will save you time, effort, and frustration. And if you want to learn more about specific organizing products and other information from The Good Housekeeping Institute, visit the *Good Housekeeping* Web site at www.goodhousekeeping.com.

So go ahead, turn the page and take your first steps toward making your home permanently clutter free!

—Ellen Levine
Editor-in-Chief
Good Housekeeping

There wasn't enough room in this kitchen for a formal pot rack, so the cooktop vent fan has been fitted with rails to hang stainless steel pans. The effect is as handsome as it is useful.

A mix of different size undercounter drawers and cabinets ensures that a variety of supplies and appliances can be efficiently stored. The drawers can also be outfitted with inserts such as cutlery organizers and pan lid slots.

Fundamentally changing bad organization habits in the kitchen and truly banishing clutter there may require moving things around quite a bit. You may also need to alter long-standing habits. So be open to the changes you'll need to make, and keep your eye on the goal—a permanently clutter-free kitchen.

Cabinets

⏱ 15–25 MINUTES (PER CABINET)

You'll begin with your cabinets. Reorganizing these will probably mean moving some things to other zones of the kitchen. Working on one cabinet at a time, pull everything out and give the shelves a quick cleaning. Now assess what you've pulled out of the cabinet. Is it food, equipment, or supplies that will be used near where the cabinet is located? If not, they should go somewhere else. Does the cabinet have a lot of extra room that is not being used efficiently? If so, the highest shelves might be best for rarely used items such as special-occasion platters. Was everything crammed into the cabinet? In this case, you'll need to find new places for much of what was there.

Take this opportunity to start shedding. Throw away open boxes of food staples that are more than 6 months old. Donate canned goods you've had for more than 9 months, because you'll probably never use them if you haven't already. (Or include the cans in your emergency preparedness kit, kept in a basement, garage, or large closet.) Discard or donate orphan glassware, dishes, or flatware whose mates have disappeared or been broken. If you still have the cartoon jelly-jar juice glasses from when your high-school-age children were toddlers, it's time to get rid of those as well—unless they're collectibles. Get rid of equipment and appliances you never use. (Remember the large electric juicer that was going to change your life and then found a permanent home behind the wine glasses? Ditch it.)

As you begin putting things back into the cupboard, group similar items together: cereals with grains, canned goods with other

Opposite: A built-in column of slide-out wood trays creates a handy in-kitchen pantry with plenty of storage space for food items large and small. Using trays or bins in a pantry helps keep odd-shaped containers in order.

STORAGE IN STYLE

CHECK YOUR BAGS: Free plastic grocery bags can save the cost of buying garbage bags, but they can be messy when stored loose under the sink or in a drawer. Get the bags under control by stuffing them in a plastic milk jug, oversized soda bottle, or an empty laundry detergent bottle that you keep under the sink, in a closet, or wherever you store cleaning supplies. Here's how: Clean the jug or bottle, cut a 2-inch hole in the side, and stuff the bags into the container. When you need a bag, just pull one out. As an alternative, keep all the bags in the bottom of your garbage pail, under the bag you're using. That way, they'll be right where you need them, when you need them. (You can also buy storage dispensers for plastic bags that mount to a cabinet door with adhesive pads or screws.)

Use a tiered cabinet organizer to organize bottled or canned goods, make the best use of cabinet space, and make it easier to find what you need.

Opposite: This colorful kitchen makes preparing food easy, with lots of workspace, handy cabinets everywhere you turn, a hanging pot rack, and organizational accents such as the spice carousel next to the cooktop.

canned goods, and glassware with dishware. This will make finding everything much easier. Get in the habit of placing all food labels facing front and lining up glassware and dishes in neat rows and stacks. The goal is to make everything in your cabinets easy to see and reach, and to make it clear where things go when the dishwasher gets emptied or bags of groceries are being put away. There should be room around glasses and appliances so you can easily remove them without having to move other items out of the way.

Larger items such as mixing bowls, waffle irons, and baking trays generally go in undercounter cabinets. But if those cabinets are crowded, consider hanging pots, pans, and any other equipment with handles or loops (see Zone 3, page 20). Or put them in the often-underutilized space above the cabinets. Consider the following unique solutions for the different types of items you plan to store in your cabinets.

➤ CANNED GOODS: Make preparing meals easier by organizing canned goods by type (for example, fruit with fruit). The trick to keeping cans organized is maintaining visibility. If you place cans of the same size one in front of the other, you can never be sure what you have—or don't have—making shopping that much more difficult. There are a number of ways to ensure that you can clearly see which canned goods are where:

Tiered shelf platforms, available in wire or solid plastic, are ideal for keeping cans and jars in plain view. Many versions are available, including those that expand, slide out, and have hideaway trays.

Helper shelves are basic wire shelves with legs. They essentially double your cabinet shelf space because you can slide cans under the shelf and place others on top of it. Some types have adjustable legs for more storage flexibility.

STORAGE IN STYLE

OUT ON A LEDGE: One way to ensure that spices are *where* you need them *when* you need them is to use a spice ledge. This is a shallow shelf no more than 2 inches deep (you can buy premade ledges or make one yourself by staining or painting and hanging a length of 1-inch-by-2-inch board). Line up your spices along the ledge with labels out and they'll be right at hand and ready for use whenever you're cooking.

Turntables or lazy Susans keep groups of items in one easily accessible place within a cupboard. For instance, place tomato sauce, paste, and canned diced tomatoes on a single shelf. Or use a two-tier lazy Susan for baby food, with vegetables and main courses on top, and fruits on the bottom.

➤ SPICES: There's no reason for a jumble of spice bottles or jars to clutter your cabinet space, especially when there are so many spice-storage options available. Put spice jars in a tiered wire or wood spice platform that lets you store them with the labels out. "Pull-down" versions can make it easier to reach the spices. A spice carousel is another option. Sometimes making sure that spices are as close as possible to the cooking area means getting them out of the cabinet; see other spice storage options in Zones 3, 4, and 7 (pages 20, 24, and 32, respectively). Regardless of where you put them, spices should be kept out of direct light and away from heat sources.

Below left: Lazy Susan trays provide quick and easy access to pots and pans, and are especially useful in hard-to-reach areas, such as the recess in these corner cabinets.

Below right: A handy, compact spice carousel fits neatly in this cabinet with plenty of room to turn to reveal the spices a cook may need.

Concealed behind a simple cabinet front, large slide-out trays organize pots and lids and contain plenty of room for bulky appliances.

➤ DRY GOODS: Boxed dry goods should be stored by type. Group breakfast cereals together, rice and beans together, and staples such as flour and sugar together. Bags of staples like dried beans, rice, and sugar are odd shapes for shelf storage. It's more space-efficient to store these in labeled see-through plastic bins or storage containers.

➤ DISHWARE AND GLASSES: Store dishware and glasses on an accessible shelf in a cupboard as close to where you'll be eating as possible. Store glasses in a row, so it's clear where they belong, and leave room around all your tableware so nothing gets broken when moving pieces in and out of the cabinet. Dishes are usually stacked, but a wire dish rack can improve access.

➤ POTS AND PANS: Cookware is usually kept in undercounter cabinets, where the pieces won't hurt anyone if they fall. But keeping them orderly is a challenge. The first line of defense against pot and pan clutter is nesting: Whenever possible, store one pot inside a larger one to reduce the amount of space they take up. Of course, you'll need to get to your cookware on an almost daily basis, so you may want to invest in a slide-out cabinet tray. When you're dealing with pots and pans, you also have the challenge of storing their lids. A simple tray or bin can serve the purpose of collecting pot lids in one place, but for roughly the same cost, you can buy a wire pot lid rack that will keep them in a neat row.

DOLLAR SMART

CLEARLY BETTER: Why spend money on storage containers for loose dry goods when you can turn to your recycling bin for free, attractive containers? Clean, clear-glass wine bottles with tight-fitting corks intact make eye-catching containers for rice, sugar, ground coffee, and other fine-textured dry goods (use a funnel to fill them). The filled containers look great, and you'll find that pouring sugar out of a bottle is much easier than pouring it out of a bag.

Undersink Space

🕐 15 MINUTES

The cabinet space under the sink often becomes a wasteland of half-filled bottles of household cleaners, loose garbage bags, and other clutter. Its odd dimensions and the presence of pipes can make this area seem nearly unusable. But the space can actually be outfitted to provide a range of storage; it's just a matter of choosing the right organizer for your needs.

An undersink stacking basket system keeps cleaning supplies in order and slides out for easy access.

To make the space as efficient as possible, create groupings under the sink. For instance, keep all household cleansers in one container, such as a bucket or carryall. That way, all the cleansers will move together, making it easy to find and use whichever you need. The same is true of poisonous household aids. (Be sure to use a child-proof cabinet lock in a kitchen where children are present.)

➤ PULLOUT STACKING BASKET SYSTEMS: You can really take advantage of available space with a pullout system of tiered baskets. Easy to get at, they can be used to store most anything you would want to put under the sink.

➤ UNDERSINK STRETCHABLE SHELVES: Designed specifically to expand to the dimensions of undersink space, the best of these can be adjusted for both width and height. They provide fairly sturdy support for bottled cleansers, detergent, and other bulky items.

Pullout towel bars make cleanup a breeze—the towels hang dry out of sight between uses and are close at hand when they're needed.

➤ SLIDE-OUT OR PULLOUT TOWEL BARS: Simple chrome rods on runners or hinges are a great way to hide towels from view most of the time, while keeping them accessible for drying dishes or cleaning counters.

➤ CABINET-DOOR-MOUNTED RACKS AND TRAYS: These put storage in a handy place—on the inside of undersink cabinet doors. Although they can be used on all cabinet doors, these types of organizers are more appropriate under the sink. The depth of the space and lack of shelving ensure the door can close, even with the storage unit in place. The units range from small wire or acrylic bins that can be used to hold sponges or dishrags to more complex, multicompartment tray systems that can store extra bottles of dish soap, scrub brushes, and more.

➤ TRAY DIVIDERS: Undersink partitions are a great use of the space for cooks with few cabinets who do a lot of baking and use cookie sheets, griddles, muffin pans, and other long, flat bakeware. The dividers can be stationary, positioned to cordon off the number of pieces you're storing, or you can purchase a higher-end unit with adjustable dividers fixed to a platform that slides out.

➤ PULLOUT GARBAGE AND RECYCLING PAILS: Some of the most useful undersink additions you can buy are dual bins mounted on smooth-action runners. They almost make taking out the trash or recycling a pleasure.

ZONE 3

Hanging Storage

🕐 15 MINUTES

Much of what clutters cabinets and drawers can be hung from the ceiling or wall. Both ceiling- and wall-mounted racks come as a simple rack, or a rack-and-shelf combination. Wall-mounted units allow more flexibility to accommodate your height and reach.

When considering hanging cookware or other kitchen necessities, look for unused wall space or areas of the ceiling over work spaces. Measure carefully and don't hang storage where it will impede work flow or get in the way of cabinet or refrigerator door swing. Ideally, anything hung in the kitchen should be in arm's reach of the shortest person who will be cooking there.

➤ RAIL SYSTEMS: Pick a hanging rail bar and then select a variety of accessories to create your own customized system. The bars are sold in different lengths, so you can make a system to fit available space. Accessories include:

- Bottle caddy (usually with two slots, ideal for oil and vinegar cruets or open bottles of red or white wine)
- Utensil hooks
- Book holder (to keep a cookbook open at eye level during food prep)
- Dish racks (can be used to store dishes or just to dry them if you don't have a dishwasher)
- Paper-towel holder
- Shelf (available as a single or double shelf)
- Corner shelf (bridges two rails on perpendicular walls)
- Hanging knife block
- Cutlery holders (usually in the shape of stainless steel cups with mesh bottoms)
- Stemware racks

Hanging rails can hold a full complement of storage accessories, from individual utensil hooks to a cookbook rack.

A basic wire grid system offers a diversity of hanging storage options in a small area.

➤ **POT RACKS:** Hang pots, pans, oven mitts, towels, and more from these handy and fashionable units. Available in an array of sizes, shapes, and materials, pot racks can supply much-needed storage, freeing up a lot of cabinet space. They also look great and let you position pots and pans near where you will use them.

➤ **HOOKS:** Ordinary hooks can be as useful in the kitchen as they are in other rooms. Hooks are good choices for places where hanging bars and racks won't fit, or where you need to hang only one or two items, such as a dish towel, oven mitt, or a string of garlic or peppers. Hooks can also keep backpacks and jackets from collecting on the kitchen table. Specialized mug hooks for undercabinet storage can provide easy access to these often-used items.

➤ HANGING BASKETS: Easily some of the most adaptable and useful hanging storage units, hanging baskets can hold many things, taking up relatively little vertical space. Placed near a food prep area, a three-tiered basket provides a place to keep fruits and root vegetables that should not be refrigerated. By the kitchen table, a single hanging basket can hold colorful napkins and place mats.

➤ HANGING GLASS RACKS: Stemware racks vary in size, from small wall-mounted units that will support eight to twelve glasses to overhead units that can hold more than twenty. You can also buy a unit with a wine-rack shelf above the glass storage, though wine is best stored in a cool, dry place.

ZONE 4

Drawers

⏱ 15 MINUTES (PER DRAWER)

Few things are as frustrating as frantically searching through an overcrowded drawer for something you know is in there somewhere. That's why the hard-and-fast rule of the organized kitchen is: no "junk" drawers. Keeping your kitchen drawers organized is simple but essential to making the kitchen as efficient as possible.

The key to keeping drawers neat and tidy is to limit them to storage by type. If you are using a drawer for phone-station storage, don't keep wine openers and serving spoons with the notepad, pencils, and takeout menus there. Keep flatware drawers free of the large utensils that belong in a dedicated drawer or should be hung up. By segregating drawer storage this way, it becomes clear to anyone in the kitchen where items go. This makes it more likely that every item will be put back where it belongs after use.

Although some islands and undercounter cabinet sets feature deep drawers suitable for appliances or larger equipment such as

ANATOMY OF A JUNK DRAWER

Dissecting your junk drawer can be a revealing exercise, with lessons for organizing the rest of the kitchen.

• **PAPERS:** Aside from recipes, coupons, and a notepad to record calls and make shopping or to-do lists, the kitchen should be a paperless place. Sift through your junk-drawer paper and throw away out-of-date documents (flyers, expired coupons, ticket stubs). Current coupons should be kept in an envelope or simple plastic wallet paper-clipped to the pad you use for shopping lists and phone messages. That way, you can reference the coupons when making your shopping list. Notes you've made and phone numbers you've jotted down should be moved to your office where they can be filed (except for an emergency phone numbers list, which should be kept in a plastic sleeve next to the phone or hung from the refrigerator with a magnet). Move takeout menus to your phone station (see Zone 5, page 26). Homework and other miscellaneous papers should be moved to their proper areas in the house.

• **UTENSILS:** Crowded drawers are hiding places for seldom-used utensils, such as a garlic press, a candy thermometer, or egg-fry rings. Utensils you use frequently should be grouped with other utensils, in containers or in drawers. Duplicates should be given away, or discarded if they are in bad shape. Those you'll never use should be given away as well.

• **OFFICE SUPPLIES:** They're called office supplies because they belong in an office. The only pens or pencils in the kitchen should be kept in the phone station. Backup note pads and sticky reminder notes should be moved to the home office or work desk. Likewise for rubber bands, paper clips, and other work-related paraphernalia.

• **CHILD'S PLAY:** Toys and other child-related items such as pacifiers, bibs, and rattles should be moved to the nursery or child's bedroom. If your children are grown, however, these items should be discarded.

• **MEDICAL SUPPLIES:** Most over-the-counter and prescription medicines should be kept in the bathroom, in the aptly named medicine cabinet. Medicines meant to be taken with meals can be placed with your vitamins in a cool, dry place out of direct light, such as a kitchen cabinet. Bandages and gauze pads should also be placed in the bathroom. If you're concerned about kitchen emergencies, mount a first-aid kit on a kitchen wall so it's easy to find when needed. Make sure to position this kit out of the reach of small children.

• **LOOSE CHANGE:** Start a "fun fund" for your children with change from the junk drawer. Take a see-through container with a mouth big enough to pass a quarter, and put the loose change in it. Empty your pockets of change each night and the kids get to see their fund grow! Keep the container in your bedroom, or wherever you empty your pockets every night.

• **HOME IMPROVEMENT LEFTOVERS:** Screws, nails, small tools, and other home improvement materials should go out to the garage or wherever you keep the household toolbox.

When you're done dissecting your junk drawer, you should have an empty space ideal for storing the things that really belong in the kitchen.

mixing bowls, most of your kitchen drawers are shallow. This makes them appropriate for storing flat items such as linens, napkins, flatware, and cutlery. But you can adapt your drawers for many other types of storage with a little help from a drawer organizer.

➤ **SPICE INSERTS:** These one-piece units have slots that hold the spice jars at an angle, making it easy to see and grab the spice you need.

➤ **FLATWARE CADDIES:** They're still the best way to keep your everyday knives, forks, and spoons in order. Choose from wire, plastic, or fancier wood types. Just make sure you get a caddy that will hold all your flatware and still fit neatly within the dimensions of your drawer.

➤ **EXPANDABLE CUTLERY ORGANIZERS:** Flexibility is the key selling point of these units. They are used for the same purpose as flatware caddies, but expand to the size of the drawer and provide more varied storage slots. This gives you spaces for steak knives, other cutlery, and utensils such as can openers, in addition to the space you need for your day-to-day flatware.

➤ **KNIFE RACKS:** If you don't want to hang knives and don't have counter space for a knife block, keep knives sharp and in order with a knife-tray drawer insert. These keep the knife blades from rubbing against other surfaces and going dull.

➤ **EXPANDABLE COMPARTMENT ORGANIZERS:** For more general drawer storage, turn to these cousins of expandable flatware organizers. Adjustable in length and width, they come with odd-sized compartments to store everything from wine openers to twist ties to straws.

➤ **INTERLOCKING ORGANIZERS:** Individual clear or white plastic compartments can be assembled in any number of combinations to create a custom storage drawer. Mix and match the compartments to accommodate changing storage needs.

Separate compartments make this drawer perfect for organizing flatware or cutlery. Choose custom-made drawers such as this for common flatware, and opt for removable compartments for odd-shaped, specialized utensils.

One of many drawer organizers available, this particular wooden insert turns a drawer into a handy spice rack with at-a-glance convenience. Before purchasing this type of organizer, be sure to count the number of spice jars you have to estimate the size organizer you will need.

A sliding top tray provides access to everyday flatware, while the bottom insert holds accessories and less frequently used utensils.

➤ ROLLING TRAY INSERTS: An unusual drawer option, these essentially provide two levels of storage for deep drawers. So, for instance, you could put accessories such as straws, birthday candles, and balloons on the bottom, and themed party utensils in the rolling tray.

➤ KITCHENWARE ORGANIZERS: If finding a good place to store your dishes is a problem, a kitchenware organizer may be the answer. You'll need a large, sturdy, deep drawer. The organizer features a baseplate with holes, and pegs that can be moved to accommodate different-sized plates.

Countertops, Work Surfaces, and Shelves

⏱ 15 MINUTES (PER COUNTER OR SHELF)

Flat, open surfaces provide the opportunity for "display" storage. So much of what is stored in the kitchen is attractive, and shelves and countertops give you a chance to use storage containers that double as decorative pieces. This lets you use your countertop to accent your decor while freeing up storage elsewhere.

Items stored on countertops and work surfaces should be confined in functional "stations." This will leave long stretches clear to serve as work surfaces whenever you need them.

➤ **PHONE STATION:** The ideal phone setup for the kitchen is a wall-mounted phone over accessible counter space. The phone station should include a "frequently called" number list with emergency numbers, a notepad of some sort, takeout menus, and a pen. If the station is next to the refrigerator, use a magnetic notepad with the pen on a cord, and use a magnetic pocket to keep menus and other papers organized. If the refrigerator isn't close, use a tray next to the phone, and keep notepad and papers confined in the tray.

➤ **WORK STATION FOR COOKING:** Clustering basic implements and ingredients you regularly use in cooking can make meal preparation quicker. Self-contained units do the trick here. Keep often-used utensils on a lazy Susan, with compartments for cooking oil, salt and pepper, and basic condiments. Position commonly used staples such

This countertop coffee station is hidden away behind an undercabinet fold-down door when not in use. Appliance "niches" allow for a streamlined look, and help you keep spills from any kitchen appliance contained.

The central island in this well-equipped kitchen serves as a food preparation work station complete with a small sink for washing fresh fruit and vegetables. A centralized workspace keeps the mess in one place and makes cleanup a breeze.

as garlic and onions next to the food-prep work station. Be sure to leave plenty of surface area for chopping, cutting, and other types of recipe preparation.

➤ FOOD STATIONS: The traditional practice of grouping certain staples in containers is as effective today as it was years ago. For instance, a countertop group of airtight canisters holding sugar, flour, coffee, and tea keeps these frequently used consumables centralized and accessible. You can create container groups of dried beans, grains and cereals, oils and vinegars.

➤ **SMALL-APPLIANCE STATION:** Unless you use a small appliance almost daily, find a place to store it off the countertop or work surface. Essential appliances such as coffeemakers and toaster ovens will need to be positioned where there is a plug. Whenever possible, buy models that mount under upper cabinets, which makes it easier to keep the counter clean and organized.

➤ **TV STATION:** If you like to have a TV in your kitchen, find a corner to tuck it in where the set will take up as little space as possible. Better still, opt for a small, fold-down undercabinet model that can be kept out of the way when it is not being used.

Shelves are versatile and useful flat-surface storage and they are available in all shapes and sizes. Buy shelving according to your needs and available wall space. Although chrome wire shelving is popular in today's kitchen, consider wood, solid metal, or plastic shelves if you need storage for tall, thin containers such as elegant oil cruets. These types of containers will be unstable on wire shelves.

Opposite: Wall-mounted shelving provides open display storage for your serving pieces and stemware.

If you have the room, an "accessory tree" can provide flexible storage. The pole can hold a number of shelves, which can be positioned exactly where you need them.

➤ **STAND-ALONE SHELVES:** An independent unit can be a quick fix for lack of storage just about anywhere in a kitchen. Tall, thin shelving units can fit in the awkward wall space between two doors, or between a door and a window. The stability of short, wide units will be handy if you need to store heavy items such as mixers, blenders, and other large appliances. It's wise to anchor taller units to the wall with a screw-in brace.

➤ **WALL-MOUNTED SHELVES:** These provide adaptable options, and are best used for "overflow" storage. For instance, if you have too many canned goods for available cabinet and pantry space, install a shelf near the pantry for extra storage. Use shelves for more immediate needs; in the case of canned goods, use the shelf rather than the pantry for foods likely to be consumed most quickly. Simple, solid shelves are also a good place to put cookbooks and other kitchen reference materials.

Refrigerator and Freezer

30 MINUTES

Keeping your refrigerator organized is one of the bigger challenges in the kitchen. Everyone in the house uses the refrigerator, and the contents change day by day. You can maintain order by being diligent about where things are put, and by establishing a logical organization within the refrigerator. (Be sure to tell your family your organization principles so they'll abide by them.)

The first order of business is weeding out obviously spoiled foods and leftovers. Then throw out any open jars, bottles, or cans that are more than 6 months old and ones that you haven't used in recent memory. You'll need to do the same weeding out of the freezer. Keep in mind that food in the freezer doesn't stop aging, it just ages

Keep your favorite canned beverage handy in a minimum of space with a simple wire grid dispenser. Besides giving you easy access to beverages, the dispenser is an economical use of refrigerator space.

THE REFRIGERATOR RULES

1. Containerize. Make loose food items (such as open packages of lunch meats and shredded cheeses) easier to store and stack by collecting them in containers. Each container should be dedicated to one food type and clearly labeled. Vegetables are an exception; they should be kept loose in the crisper.

2. Assign shelf space. When unpacking groceries or returning leftovers to the refrigerator, it's easy to slip into the habit of just putting things wherever you see space. This makes for a disorganized jumble that will lead to spoilage, waste, and frustration. Assign different types of food (such as dairy or prepared meals) to their own sections of the fridge. If you have a large family or a large fridge, use labels so everyone knows which area is which.

3. Rotate. This key practice prevents food waste in restaurants and is just as effective for homes. Whenever you put a new item, such as a carton of milk, in the refrigerator, move any old one in front of it so that the old one is consumed first.

This lazy Susan is ideal for refrigerator storage. Made of cleanable plastic, the molded lip contains spills and the small size is perfect for making crowded refrigerator shelves more accessible. The ability to rotate the unit allows you to grab what you need without having to reach far into the refrigerator.

very slowly. If you have food in the freezer that is more than 9 months old, throw it out. Now give the whole unit a thorough cleaning and you're ready to put everything back according to assigned locations.

➤ PACKAGED FOOD: Grouping food in distinct areas can be tough because the refrigerator layout is usually pretty open. Use transparent covered bins for bags of food, such as shredded cheese, open packages of premium coffee, and other loose foods. Keep bottled condiments together in the door slot. Other packaged foods, such as coffee beans or ground coffee, should be kept together in trays, which contain spills and make it obvious what goes where.

➤ BEVERAGES: Soda bottles have a tendency to tip on wire shelves, so if your refrigerator has wire shelves, buy a piece of Plexiglas at the local hardware store (have it cut to size) to serve as a platform for the soda bottles and other tall, unsteady containers. Canned beverages such as beer and soda should be organized in a wire can-dispenser. Inexpensive and simple in design, these dispensers—for those who drink a lot of canned beverages—hold twelve or more cans, take up a minimum of space, and use a gravity feed

THE INSIDE SCOOP

QUALITY CONTROL: Keeping refrigerated food fresh for as long as possible is simply a matter of knowing what goes where.

• *Cheeses:* Semisoft cheeses can be kept in the freezer for up to a year, and hard cheeses for almost two, but they must be tightly wrapped.

• *Eggs:* Keep eggs in their container and not in the door; this way they'll stay fresh longer. The carton helps maintain proper egg temperature and keeps the eggs from absorbing refrigerator odors.

• *Potatoes, onions, and garlic:* Keep these outside the refrigerator because the excess moisture degrades their quality.

system to neatly dispense one can at a time. If you're a fan of sports drinks and buy several bottles at once, refrigerate only one at a time—keep the rest in another location, such as the pantry.

➤ **LEFTOVERS:** You should also have a distinct area for leftovers, so you and your family know where to find them. Of course, if you're running low on room and the leftovers may spoil before use, it's wiser to freeze them.

ZONE 7

Pantry

 30 MINUTES

A pantry is your kitchen's warehouse. Simple in design and principle, a pantry is a self-contained area for open storage. The space lets you stock up on staples and provides a dedicated location for backups of common household items, from extra boxes of coffee filters to a supply of paper towels. If you're fortunate enough to have a built-in pantry as part of your home, the challenge is to make sure it's well organized. But even if a pantry isn't part of your home's layout, you can usually create a pantry space in your

Opposite: A prefab shelf system can be the ideal way to turn an alcove into a spacious pantry. All the shelves and drawers in this installation are adjustable, allowing the design to change as supplies and storage needs change.

THE PANTRY RULES

1. **Take stock.** A pantry should be used as backup storage so you have extras of everything you need on hand.

2. **Organize by level.** The order of items on pantry shelves depends on how often you need them. Long-term storage of backup items goes on bottom shelves. The most commonly used dry goods are placed at eye level. Items that are rarely used, such as fuel canisters for a fondue set, go on the highest shelves, out of everyday reach.

3. **No perishables.** Pantries should be used for dry goods and staples with a long shelf life. Foods that might spoil if left out in the open for a few days need to go in the refrigerator or near the food-preparation area.

Above: Turn a tiny broom closet into a full-service pantry with this space-expanding wire shelf system. Easy to install and to keep clean, it slides out on runners.

Right: Keep a busy kitchen well stocked, with a stand-alone pantry. This piece of furniture has amazing capacity with its swing-out doors and pullout compartments. When shut, it looks like a set of cabinets.

kitchen. To prevent clutter and waste, there should be a logic to what you put in the pantry and where you locate it.

➤ **DRY GOODS:** Airtight bags of flour, sugar, rice, tea, and other dry foods in bulk are well suited for storage in the pantry. As a space-saving alternative, use containers that fit your shelves perfectly.

➤ **PAPER GOODS:** Take advantage of pantry space to buy paper goods in bulk. Even though backup items generally go on bottom shelves, position paper goods close to the top of the pantry so they can't be damaged by errant spills.

➤ **BEVERAGES:** Most beverages can be stored in a cool, dry pantry space for a significant period of time. This frees up refrigerator space and lets you buy beer and soda at case prices. Keep the beverages in their cases for most efficient storage.

➤ **COOKBOOKS:** Because the pantry is usually set apart from the messy part of the kitchen, it can be a perfect place to store cookbooks. If you don't have a pantry, keep the most frequently used cookbooks handy in the kitchen and move the rest to bookshelves elsewhere in the house.

There are many ways to fabricate a pantry, from putting adjustable shelves or a freestanding shelving unit within the closet, to buying one of the many prefab pantry systems. Whether you make your own or buy a premade pantry system, look for flexibility, such as adjustable shelves. You should be able to change the configuration of the pantry based on changing storage needs.

A pullout, wire-grid storage system lets you convert a ceiling-height cabinet or a small broom closet into a new kitchen pantry. Individual shelves in these systems can be arranged to accommodate different-height items. You can also buy accessory grids designed to hold pot lids and other utensils. You can opt for pullout, solid trays that will hold many different containers firmly in place.

ZONE 8

Kitchen Table

🕐 15 MINUTES

Your kitchen table is usually the central gathering place in the kitchen. It tends to fill multiple roles, from a social center to a place for eating meals to a desk for reading. Because so much goes on around the kitchen table, clutter is a natural problem. You can beat clutter and the general disorganization of table space by "centerpiecing" whatever is stored on the table and by keeping the table prepared for meals.

Centerpiecing is simply creating a central area—on a mini lazy Susan or in some other type of small organizer such as a basket—where all the items that will be permanently kept on the table are collected and organized. Put the basics—salt, pepper, napkins—in the centerpiece, leaving a small amount of space for other condiments

A lazy Susan centralizes food and condiments during meals and basics such as salt and pepper at other times.

during mealtime. Use bowls around this centerpiece as necessary to keep fruit or other treats for the family on hand.

Keep the table covered with a simple tablecloth or lay out place mats, and you'll be able to keep the table free of homework and bills.

KEEPING UP

Even after you've put all your organizational changes in place, you'll need to remain vigilant to the accumulation of clutter. Because so much happens in the kitchen, implement these strategies to ensure clutter doesn't become a problem again.

• **Empty sink, closed doors:** Make a habit of emptying the kitchen sink every night and closing all open cabinet doors. The simple act of putting dishes in the dishwasher or washing them by hand, and making sure doors and drawers are closed, makes clutter on counters and cabinets stand out. Deal with this clutter every night; a quick pickup is far easier than tackling a big cleaning.

• **Weekly bin run:** If the kitchen table is a recurrent clutter hot spot, keep a small decorative bin or tray on a shelf or counter near the table. Each night, put anything that doesn't belong on the table in the bin. At the end of the week, whichever family member has the most items in the bin must empty it by putting everything back where it belongs. (Other family members may need to tell "the winner" where particular items go.) After a few weeks, the entire family will want to avoid the responsibility of the bin and will see the upside to keeping the kitchen table clutter free.

• **Fridge weeding:** The inside of your refrigerator can too easily become a case of "out of sight, out of mind." This presents a particular kitchen challenge because your food inventory is always changing. Assign 1 day every 2 weeks for fridge weeding. The process should take no more than 10 minutes if you do it regularly. Remove and discard leftovers, fruits, vegetables, and dairy products that are past their prime. Then make sure that the oldest items are placed in the front of the refrigerator, and that you're sticking to the other guidelines in Zone 6.

CHAPTER 2 | Bedrooms and Kids' Rooms

Bedrooms are the most personal spaces in a home, functioning as private hideaways. These rooms are all about comfort and seclusion, offering a place to relax and recharge your batteries. In addition to sleeping and romance, you may use your bedroom for other restful activities such as reading or watching TV. The bedroom is also a highly functional space; it's where you dress and get ready to face the day. But no matter what you're doing in your bedroom, it will be easier, more enjoyable, and more refreshing if the space is neat and orderly.

The most obvious source of clutter in the bedroom is clothing. Your clothing changes over time with the season and the whims of fashion. But your closet space and the way it is organized often does not change. This means that much of what you wear probably doesn't have a proper place in your closet, or is stored haphazardly, making the closet crowded and untidy. The result is an alarming jumble of clothes. The solution lies in reorganizing the closet to accommodate what actually needs to go there, and moving what doesn't.

Bedroom furniture and accessories also play a part in how easy it is to dress or undress without leaving a trail of clothes. Something as simple as a well-organized jewelry box with separate compartments for earrings, rings, and necklaces can make dressing quicker. It will also keep the top of your dresser clutter free. Used effectively, your bedroom furniture can provide short- and long-term storage, and can free up much-needed closet space.

Organize the zones in this room in order: closets, bedside and bed, dresser, suspended storage (hooks and shelves), and accessory furniture. Certain things now stored in one zone will need to move to the next zone to free up space. For instance, it might make sense

Opposite: This simple and elegant bedroom uses a few wisely chosen furnishings. The modest nightstand leaves little space for clutter.

Furnishing a clutter-reducing bedroom means limiting where things can be put. This simple bedroom includes smart furniture and accents that beautify while they simplify.

A mounted reading light saves space on a nightstand, allowing it to be more compact.

This nightstand is ideal for a streamlined bedroom; having no drawers and a tray top limits what can be put on it. A vase, an alarm clock, and a picture fill the space nicely.

The modest bench is useful for laying out tomorrow's clothes, and as a surface for a folded blanket or two. The minimal area and slotted surface fight clutter, too.

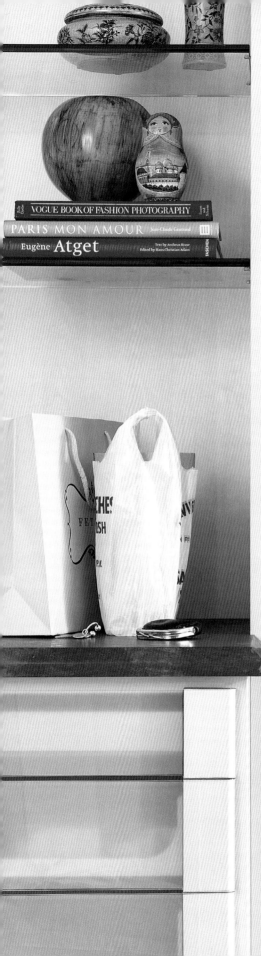

VOGUE BOOK OF FASHION PHOTOGRAPHY

PARIS MON AMOUR   Jean-Claude Gautrand

Eugène **Atget**

Text by Andreas Krase
Edited by Hans Christian Adam
TASCHEN

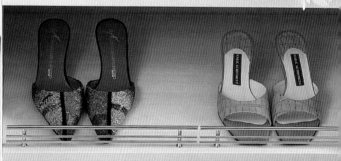

STORAGE IN STYLE

BASKET CASE: So much of what you need to store in the bedroom is soft and easy to fold or roll, which makes baskets a natural choice for keeping things tidy. Baskets also make beautiful display containers that let you keep all kinds of garments out in the open. Use wicker or reed baskets to hold rolled towels or folded sweaters. Use smaller woven baskets for scarves and gloves. You can use baskets with tops if you prefer a neat and tidy appearance, or leave the baskets topless to let your textiles add color to the room.

to take the extra comforter out of the closet to make sufficient room for your clothes. The comforter might be better suited for underbed storage, or in a chest at the foot of the bed.

When considering the times listed for each zone, realize that they take into account a two-person bedroom. If you are the only person using your bedroom, you can expect to spend less time on each zone.

The idea is for you to become flexible about where things go, letting common sense and practicality guide you. An appropriate mix of storage areas, and making the most of those areas, will go a long way toward maintaining the bedroom as your own orderly sanctuary. In addition, always be sure to put magazines, mail, photos, and so on in their proper zones in other rooms; don't leave them strewn about the bedroom.

ZONE 1

Closets

1 HOUR

Opposite: An ideal closet configuration includes assorted types of storage to accommodate different types of clothing, shoes, accessories, and other personal items. Here, handbags, folded shirts, and other attractive soft garments find a home on spacious wood shelves.

Your bed may be the centerpiece of rest and relaxation, but your closet is the cornerstone of bedroom organization. If you're constantly searching for your favorite shirt or dress, can't find matching shoes, or are stumbling over clothes on your way out of the room, the closet is probably to blame. Fortunately, closets are fairly easy to organize, and stores offer a wealth of products to help you do just that. In fact, the options available ensure that no matter what size your closet is, you will find custom shelving, hanging bars, fixtures, and other organizers that will precisely meet your needs within the constraints of your available closet space.

You can choose from a long list of innovative closet-organizing accessories. These include shoe-cubby shelves, specialized multigarment hangers, belt racks, revolving tie racks, wall- or pole-hung canvas shelves, and more. You can also opt for a completely new, customized closet system, designed by one of the many companies specializing in closet organization.

The first step in making the most of your closet is assessing the space. Remove everything in the closet and measure the actual dimensions. You'll use these measurements to determine what kind of storage should go where, as well as for purchasing any type of closet-organizing system or elements.

Next comes the shedding process. Go through what you've removed, and weed out the clothes and other things you should get rid of, and remove anything in the closet that is more logically stored elsewhere, including clothes that are out of season, which should be stored. Now you're ready to organize what remains.

➤ HANGING STORAGE: try to limit the amount of clothes that will be hung, because folded clothes take up less space. Most pants—even dress slacks—can be carefully folded. Button-down shirts can be buttoned and folded as department stores do for display. This makes

Tall piles of soft clothes have a way of tipping over and getting jumbled. A simple set of stacking shelves can help keep soft clothes organized and avoid unnecessary wear and tear on your garments.

THE CLOSET RULES

1. Hang less. Many of the clothes you are in the habit of hanging up can be stored folded, taking up far less space. Folded items can be placed in a range of locations, including shelves out in the open, closet shelves, drawers, and bins and baskets.

2. Be flexible. Because your clothing requirements change over time, your closet should have as many flexible features as possible.

3. Group by type. Keep similar clothes together—dress shirts with dress shirts, jeans with jeans, and so on—and they will be easy to locate when you want to wear them.

it easy to see the shirt you want and keeps them in a neat stack. Decide which garments absolutely must be hung, such as business suits and blouses, and group them by how much hanging space they'll need—long or short. Now you have a good idea of how long each closet rod must be. Look to optimize your hanging storage (while being careful not to overload the rod with too much weight for the supports you are using). If you have extra space on a closet rod holding long dresses and bathrobes, use a "stacking hanger" with several bars to hold a number of pairs of pants in limited horizontal space. Although you may want to use hanging accessories such as rod-mounted tie or belt racks and hanging shelves, it's usually wiser to reserve hanging space for clothes on hangers.

Varied lengths of hanging storage are essential for making a closet as orderly as possible. This setup accommodates folded pants and suit coats, medium-length dresses, and full-length garments.

THE INSIDE SCOOP

HANGING AROUND: When clothes are given the appropriate amount of space in the closet, they are easier to remove and replace, making dressing and undressing easier. The right amount of space also keeps the clothes wrinkle free and reduces unnecessary wear and tear. The proper horizontal spacing lets you easily pass your hand between garments hanging next to each other. Here are general guidelines for the vertical space you should allow for different clothes (measured from hanging bar to top of surface below it, such as the floor, another hanging bar, or a shelf):

45 inches	Suits, dress shirts, blouses, sports jackets, other jackets
35 inches	Trousers folded over hangers, ties
70 inches	Dresses, gowns, bathrobes, trousers hung full length

➤ **SHELVING:** Closet shelves should always be adjustable to allow for changing storage needs. Shelves can be used to store everything from shoes to hat boxes to folded clothes and more. Anything you put on shelves should be grouped with like items—all sweaters together, all shoes in a row, and so on. Wire shelving is widely available in preset widths, and is usually sold with matching brackets or as part of a complete closet system. Wire shelving can also be cut to your desired width, giving you a lot of latitude in customizing closet storage. This type of shelving is fairly inexpensive and is fine for holding boxes and other flat items. However, wire construction may leave lines on folded soft clothing, and will allow loose objects to fall through. Often, the better choice is laminate or wood shelving. Laminate shelving comes in a range of set widths and depths, and is supported on tracks that let you move the shelves as needed. Wood shelves offer a nicer look, and can be cut to suit specific measurements. If you are going to stack clothes such as sweaters or pants, use enough shelves in the column to ensure you don't stack more than three or four garments on a pile.

A column of shelves can serve as a basic divider for a his-and-hers closet. Clearly marked borders for a closet with two users are crucial to contain and defeat clutter.

A busy professional couple requires a well-organized closet, and this design meets their needs admirably. A variety of hanging storage options is augmented with shoe cubbies, shelves, cabinets for oversized items, and abundant drawers.

Clothes stacked higher are apt to slide or fall off the pile and become messy. For ultimate convenience, choose plastic or laminate shelves that slide in and out of grooves cut in the side supports.

➤ CONCEALED STORAGE: Depending on the size of your closet, you may opt to include drawers or pullout trays for organizing smaller items. Drawer units can easily be integrated into just about any closet layout. A closet drawer or bin is ideal for a range of storage, from a stash of daily contact lenses to spare eyeglasses and watches. The drawer cabinet for a closet is usually shallower than a

THE INSIDE SCOOP

FENCED OFF: Long shelves can easily fall into disarray as piles of clothes or shoes become jumbled together over time. Consider using a partition on long shelves. These accessories clip or screw onto the shelf, dividing the shelf into compartments that contain different items in their own spaces.

THE INSIDE SCOOP

OFFICE SPACE: Open up room in your closet by keeping the shoes you wear only at work, at work. Keep those shoes in a bottom drawer of your desk, or in a large box with a lid, placed on a shelf.

BORDER PATROL: Sharing closet space—even with a loved one—can be a trying experience. As you organize your closet, create a border between your storage and your partner's. The border can be the vertical board that holds the support for hanging rods or a column of shelves. Because women tend to have more clothes and need more closet space than men, organize the woman's side of the closet first.

dresser drawer, and is mounted on the same vertical brace that holds the hanging poles (or on brackets, like other closet fixtures). Most closet drawers have dividers to create separate compartments within the drawer. There are also many specialized drawers and pullouts with compartments specifically designed to hold handkerchiefs, scarves, pantyhose, socks, belts, or other loose clothing and items. If you can include as many drawers or cabinets in your closet as you need, you may even be able to do without a regular dresser, freeing up space in the bedroom.

➤ **SHOE STORAGE:** Shoes are a special case in the closet. If kept on the floor of the closet, they are likely to get stepped on. They will often be clumped in a messy heap, making finding the shoes you want to wear difficult. A quick, easy, and inexpensive solution is a simple wire shoe rack. This keeps shoes up off the floor, slanted at an angle so you can quickly find the pair you want. You can also keep shoes on a shelf. If you're installing a complete closet system, choose a cubbyhole shelf with slots for each pair of shoes. Store each pair of shoes heel to toe, making it easier to see and grab the pair you want. Alternatively, put shoes in a canvas or plastic hanging shoe holder. Different types can be mounted on a wall, a closet rod, or the back of a door, and let you simply slip pairs of shoes in the pockets. For the easiest access, keep shoes grouped together

An overdoor hanging shoe rack is a great way to add abundant shoe storage that saves space in the closet.

Opposite: A hanging canvas shoe organizer keeps shoes from cluttering the closet floor, and provides a handy space for each pair. Organize by type of shoe to make pairs easy to locate when you are in a rush.

based on use (for example, dress shoes with dress shoes, casual wear with casual wear, and so on).

➤ DOOR STORAGE: Sliding doors don't provide any storage opportunities. But if you are willing to replace sliding closet doors with hinged double doors, you'll increase the storage potential of the closet. A variety of organizers clip onto the top of swinging doors to add storage on the inside surface, including over-the-door closet rods that provide more places to hang clothes, utility racks that can support many different types of clothes (from hats to coats to shirts on hangers), shoe racks, tie racks, and simple multipurpose hooks. Hinged, foldout hanger racks let you hang a column of pants flush against the door. Dowel racks attached to the inside face of the door let you position your tie collection at eye level.

THE CLOTHES QUESTIONS

When it comes to your wardrobe, the more streamlined the better. We tend to hold onto clothes even when we've outgrown them or they're long out of style. To make sure the clothes you have are the clothes you wear, ask yourself the following questions. Be brutally honest and you'll quickly figure out what can stay and what needs to go.

Is the article more than two sizes too big or too small? If so, you should give it away. The drastic change your body would have to undergo for the clothes to fit properly will likely take months, if it happens at all.

Has it been more than a year since you wore the piece? Older pieces often don't match new clothes we buy. These "orphans" just don't fit with your wardrobe, so donate them.

Upon close inspection, are the clothes in bad condition? Even clothes that fit look bad on you if they are threadbare. If you've found worn or frayed areas on a garment, discard or donate it.

Have you changed careers or left a line of work? If so, you may have perfectly nice (and expensive) clothes that you no longer need and won't be wearing. Donate them to charity.

Bedside and Bed

30 MINUTES

The territory around your bed—including the bed itself and your nightstands—is your comfort area. The storage in this zone, and the way things are organized, should be all about putting you at ease. If you're a reader, there should be a place to put books or magazines when not being read, and enough room for a good reading light. If you like to sleep with the scent of flowers around you, your nightstand surface should be large enough to hold a vase of flowers.

We tend to think of our furniture as permanent, but if your nightstands are too large or too small, they are part of the clutter problem and should be replaced. However, the problem may lie in what you are trying to keep in or on the nightstand. If there is no space on the surface, remove everything but what's essential to your use and enjoyment of the bed area.

➤ **NIGHTSTANDS:** Your needs should determine your nightstand, not the other way around. The right nightstand works well with your bed. The top surface should be easy to reach from the bed height. If your nightstand is too tall or too short, it will make basic tasks harder, such as setting your alarm or turning a reading light on or off. If the nightstand is too large it will invite clutter, and if it's too small, the basics you need won't fit comfortably on top. Ideally, the top of the nightstand should be large enough to hold a book, a light, and an alarm clock (and a vase and eyeglasses, if you require them). The nightstand should also have a drawer to conceal items that would detract from your bedroom decor, such as prescription medicines, the television remote, and a small flashlight. If you have a number of medications or other items you use while in bed, consider a nightstand with multiple drawers. A shelf underneath is useful for holding magazines and books to

Opposite: Clutter-beating nightstands are both compact and functional, and this glass-and-iron side table has been adapted nicely. The small top and lack of drawers limit places for clutter to hide, but there's still enough room for a vase, a tin with note-taking supplies, a lamp, and a saucer that doubles as a place to keep favorite pieces of jewelry.

STORAGE IN STYLE

EXCESS BAGGAGE: You can put your luggage to work even when you're not traveling. Use traditional case luggage as underbed storage containers for seasonal clothes and bed linens such as flannel sheets. For real flair, pick up vintage luggage at yard sales, thrift shops, or flea markets, clean it well, and use it as underbed storage.

Opposite: A guest bed with built-in drawers of various sizes leaves plenty of room for bed linens—and visitor's clothing—making a dresser unnecessary.

A small table makes for an unconventional but useful nightstand. The table has no bottom shelves or drawers that might collect clutter, and it provides all the surface area needed for the bed area.

be read. If an item is not used while you are in bed, it doesn't belong anywhere on or in the nightstand.

➤ THE BED: All beds—with the exception of completely solid platform beds—provide the opportunity for valuable long-term storage. The space under a bed is expansive and there are a number of ways to put it to good use. First, determine what type of long-term storage you need: Bulky items like comforters need a taller container than flat, compact items such as sheets. Measure how much clearance you have between the bottom of your bed and the floor, then choose a type of underbed storage that suits the space and the degree of accessibility you require. For instance, backup pillows and sheets that you use every few weeks might best be stored in a container with wheels, to make getting to them easier. Depending

One of the many types of underbed storage boxes, this plastic shoe organizer zips completely closed to keep out dust and dirt, and slides neatly under the bed.

on which type of underbed storage you choose, you may want to use a bed skirt to conceal the container.

Base drawers are prefab units that slide independently under the bed or create a foundation for the box spring or mattress. They are usually attached around the existing frame. Most often made of wood, these units create the appearance that your bed is sitting on a platform with drawers. The drawers provide a neat, finished look that stylishly conceals what you're storing. The downside to underbed drawer sets is their expense and the fact that the frame construction takes up some of the usable underbed storage space.

Simple underbed boxes are inexpensive storage options. These come in a range of shapes and materials, including durable plastic boxes that let you see the contents, wire-mesh units that allow air to circulate around whatever you're storing, and simple canvas "bags" that zip up around a metal or wood frame, completely enclosing and hiding the contents. *Rolling boxes and trays* are ideal for storing those things that you need to use more often, such as sweaters. Choose from rolling plastic containers with casters and snap-shut lids, stylish wicker boxes on wheels, open wire-mesh units, and rolling plastic frames with sliding drawers.

Dresser

30 MINUTES

The dresser provides two types of storage: concealed places to hide underwear, socks, and other clothing and valuables, and an open, accessible top surface for a jewelry box, family pictures, or other visually attractive elements. The challenge is to make certain that the dresser does not become the parking place for the random clutter that seems to migrate to the bedroom, such as mail or car keys.

Begin by removing everything in and on top of the dresser. Use this opportunity to weed out frayed bras and underwear that you no longer wear, socks and handkerchiefs with holes in them, and other

Small loose items can make a mess of a dresser top. Organizers such as the mug and silver cup used here keep small cosmetic supplies and other items under control.

An unorthodox layout keeps a small bedroom tidy and efficient. The dresser—which serves as a nightstand—has been positioned next to the bed. The reading light, book, and vase take up most of the surface space so that nothing more can be put on it.

garments that are no longer usable. Also get rid of small bits and pieces that you might have been holding onto for no good reason, such as orphaned cuff links. Move items that don't belong in the dresser, such as playing cards, sunglasses, or family pictures waiting to be framed.

What's left will be a combination of clothing and possibly items of value that have no other logical place to go. That's okay. The dresser should serve as a central storage area for undergarments, and can also house valuables that you want to keep but won't necessarily be using or even looking at on a regular basis. These can include mementos such as medals and awards, seldom-used jewelry such as tie tacks and cuff links, extra shoelaces, and other similar items. The trick to permanent dresser organization is to give everything that goes in or on the dresser a set place, even if you have to create one with special dividers or independent compartments such as boxes. Then put back all the clothing you'll store in the drawers, which will reveal how much extra storage space you have.

➤ **DRAWERS:** As with the closet, all the clothes you keep in the dresser should be neatly grouped by type. With some of your clothing, this is easy: It's a simple matter to fold men's underwear and place it in rows. Women's undergarments are a little more of an organizational challenge, and should be kept to one section of the drawer using a divider, a box, or a see-through bag. If much of what you want to store is loose goods, turn to drawer inserts. Specialized inserts are available for everything from earrings and necklaces to rolled ties and folded handkerchiefs. You can also mix and match independent plastic or wood compartments. Some plastic compartments snap together, letting you customize your drawer design.

This dresser unit is a part of the closet system. It helps fight clutter by keeping all clothing in one area.

STORAGE IN STYLE

JEWELRY STORAGE: Organizing the bits and pieces of a jewelry collection is always a challenge. If you don't have a jewelry box, or if the one you have is inadequate, consider a hideaway alternative. A small plastic toolbox can be ideal—the many different shapes and depths of the compartments let you separate pieces so they remain untangled and easy to pick out. For an even simpler solution, use ice-cube trays.

➤ **DRESSER TOP:** There are certain items best suited for the top of the dresser. Cosmetics may be essential if you do your makeup in a mirror over the dresser. An heirloom jewelry box is lovely displayed on the dresser, and provides a place for your accessories. Whatever is on top of the dresser should be self-contained. Jewelry should be kept in a jewelry box. Cosmetics should be placed on a decorative tray or in a box or cosmetics bag to prevent them from migrating. Every dresser top should have some sort of valet and a change keeper. The valet can be as formal as a wood tray with separate compartments, or as informal as a woven basket. Whatever you choose as a valet, that's where all small "pocket" clutter should be placed: cell phone, keys, money clip, wallet, and anything else you regularly carry. The change keeper is the place to put all your loose change when you empty your purse or pockets. This can be a decorative bowl, a vintage bank, or even a wide-mouthed bottle. The point is to create a set place for all the loose items that might otherwise clutter the top of the dresser. (If you have small children, be sure that your dresser has safety straps to secure the dresser frame to a wall stud, along with safety catches on the drawers.)

Right: A soft jewelry case trimmed in leather is attractive enough for the top of your dresser, but can easily be stowed away in a dresser drawer if you want to keep the top neat and bare.

Far right: Jewelry tray inserts make a jewelry box out of a dresser drawer. Lined in velvet, they keep jewelry from scratching and keep it organized in any of various sized compartments.

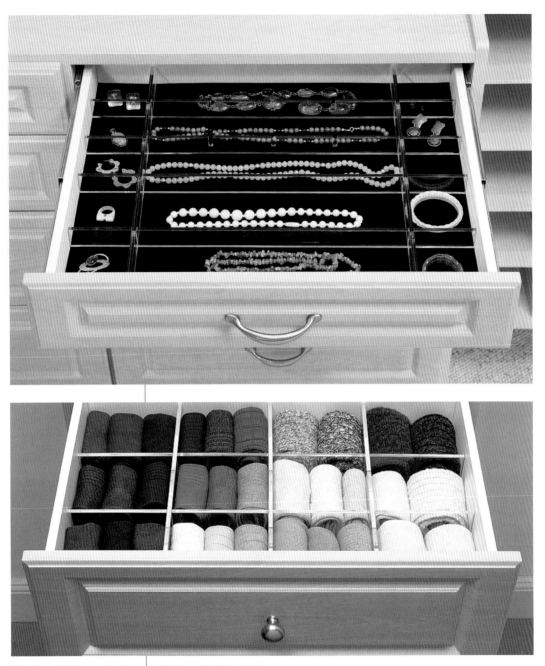

Top: Special inserts help keep closet drawers neat and valuables in order. This drawer includes a black felt lining and dividers that ensure jewelry is always right at hand.

Bottom: Built-in dividers create uniform compartments in this drawer, ideal for ties or rolled-up dress socks.

ZONE 4

Suspended Storage— Hooks and Shelves

30 MINUTES

Suspended storage is all about "hiding in plain view." Because so much of what you need to store or organize in the bedroom is pleasing to the eye, using hooks and shelves can be your chance to organize and decorate at the same time. When you use shelves and hooks you free up room elsewhere in the bedroom, and make whatever you store easier to find.

Make the most of the display nature of this type of storage. Store pretty, loose items like scarves or gloves on shelves or hang them elegantly from a row of hooks. Roll ties up tightly and arrange them in a shallow tray on a shelf.

You can choose between complete stand-alone shelving units and single shelves that are attached directly to the wall. Hooks come in sets, alone, or in variations such as pegs. Always keep in mind that flexibility is key to how useful any storage—including shelving units—will be.

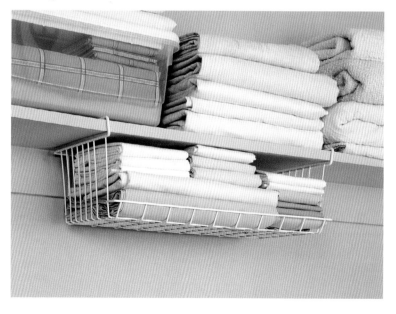

Increase the capacity of closet shelves quickly, easily, and inexpensively with undershelf bins that slide right into place.

Overdoor organizers come in many different sizes and shapes to suit a range of garments and accessories. This unit provides a flush, stable rack for ties and belts.

➤ **STAND-ALONE SHELVING:** Independent shelving units offer a lot of storage space in one unit. They can also easily be moved when necessary, and are a good choice where you have significant wall space. As elsewhere in the bedroom, organize anything you put on a shelf by type (books in a group, boxed items in a group, and so on).

➤ **ATTACHED SHELVES:** Like their stand-alone relatives, single shelves and brackets are available in just about any finish you could want, from metal to wire to all kinds of wood and plastic. Although attractive because of their price, wire shelves tend to look inexpensive, and will let small objects pass through. A solid shelf is usually a better idea in the bedroom. Position the shelf near where what you're storing will be used. Multicolored folded clothing is ideal for attached shelving. Stacks of pretty sweaters create a dynamic focal point at eye level, and ensure that you'll never have to search through a jumble of clothes for your favorite sweater again. You can prevent loose articles from falling off the end of the shelf with a shelf-end stop. This device clamps to the end of the shelf and creates a border like a bookend.

➤ **HOOKS:** Useful and versatile, hooks serve as either permanent or temporary resting places for bedroom garments and accessories. Hook sets comprise a series of hooks attached to a backing, which is hung on a wall. These are useful when you're hanging a group of similar items, such as all your scarves, purses, or belts. Single hooks are simple solutions that can easily be installed right where you want them: on the back of the bedroom door for your bathrobe, on an interior closet wall to hold a favorite pair of suspenders, or next to the dresser to hang the necklaces you wear most often. Peg sets are are helpful, too. For instance, if a collection of baseball caps seems to be forever getting in your way, install a row of pegs at the top of a wall, but within reach, to create a display of the hats.

STORAGE IN STYLE

CUBE-ISM: A great way to add hidden storage with flair is to mount cube shelves—square shelves made from four pieces of wood that form a frame—on a wall and cover their openings with fabric flaps, such as canvas, muslin, or velvet. The flaps are attached with top hinges. Choose a fabric that complements your bedroom's decor, or paint or stain the fabric to suit your design tastes. The storage will be concealed and the shelf can be placed exactly where you want, with a minimum of time and effort.

ZONE 5

Accessory Furniture

1 HOUR

Depending on the size of your bedroom, you may have room for other furnishings. These can function as overflow storage for the other zones in the bedroom, or may just be pieces you want to include to create a reading area. Whatever the case, any additional piece of furniture should have a distinct purpose to avoid becoming clutter itself—it should never interrupt the traffic flow through and around the room—and to avoid becoming a clutter magnet.

➤ **CHESTS AND TRUNKS:** Not only are they interesting additions to the room's decor, chests and trunks also provide useful long-term storage. Choose a style that suits your tastes, from an old steamer trunk to a contemporary cedar hope chest. But also let size guide your selection. If you want to store family memorabilia under thick

An antique-style armoire is the perfect hiding place for an entertainment center in this large bedroom. If you must have electronics in the bedroom, make sure they are all contained in one enclosed space.

Opposite: Shelves over a low-slung bedroom dresser are used to display an elegant vase and photos, but could just as easily be used for storing essentials such as boxes of accessories.

blankets, look for a deep chest with no auxiliary compartments or inserts. If you are storing frequently used guest linens with seasonal sweaters, look for a trunk with a tray or other compartment to separate the two types of storage. The other advantage of this type of furniture is that the lid provides a resting place for more frequently used items such as bathrobes or books, or you can use it as a place to sit while dressing. Of course, only include a chest or trunk in the room if you have genuine long-term storage needs; decorative chests have a way of collecting clutter.

➤ CHAIRS AND TABLES: If the bedroom can accommodate it, a good reading chair is a lovely addition. Keep the chair in a corner out of the flow of traffic. Along with the chair, you may want a small table. The table should only be large enough to accommodate a book and a cup of tea. Use a good standing lamp and your reading area will be complete.

➤ ENTERTAINMENT CENTERS: Although your home entertainment area should ideally be confined to a family or living room, you may opt to create a small entertainment center in your bedroom. If you do this, keep it as contained as possible. Try to position the TV and peripherals such as a DVD player or VCR in a recess (on a shelf), so that their top surfaces don't become a place for more clutter. Run cables secured to baseboards with nail-in clips, to keep them out of the way. Use a remote caddy or similar dedicated container for the remote so that it doesn't get lost between pillows on the bed or slide down between the dresser and the wall. Any DVDs or videos you bring into the bedroom

A little bedroom desk nestled in a small alcove next to the bed provides a place to read, write, and keep a log, with drawers to manage keepsakes.

should be kept in a specified container. A portable box is ideal because it serves as a place to keep the disks and you can carry it between the bedroom and your family room.

➤ **DESKS:** Normally, the zone system calls for keeping any desk in a separate home office. But a small writing or reading desk positioned in the bedroom may be more convenient for your purposes. Try to keep the top of the desk as pristine as possible; that way, any clutter that finds its way to the desk will stick out like a sore thumb. If the desk has drawers, use them to store simple writing implements and to hold other items that would normally crowd the top of the desk. Use a chair that will slide all the way under the desk so that it is out of the way of traffic flow and won't become a parking place for clothing.

KEEPING UP

Because of the relaxed nature of a bedroom, it's easy to allow things to slowly become disorganized again. It may be that you brought in a stack of catalogs to look through and were just too tired to read them right away. Or perhaps your wardrobe has expanded beyond the confines of your closet. A little periodic maintenance goes a long way toward a spotless, comfortable bedroom.

• **Culling closets:** Every 3 months or so, do a closet check. Remove older items that you no longer wear, or that were replaced by new additions to your wardrobe. Reorganize garments by type if they have gotten mixed up in the process of cleaning and rehanging or refolding.

• **Drawer check:** Once each month, right after you do the laundry, take a minute while you're putting away underwear and socks to ensure that your dresser is as organized as it should be. Are like items grouped together? Is it simple to find exactly what you need? Are there any loose items on top of the dresser that need to find a home? Straighten up as necessary to keep the dresser a functional, tidy zone.

• **Bedside scan:** Get in the habit of making a weekly visual sweep of the bed and surrounding area. Remove anything that shouldn't be there, and make sure your nightstand is as neat and organized as it was when you first finished the zone.

Kids' Rooms

The term "kid's room" has several different meanings, depending on the age of the child. Obviously, the decor and organization of a toddler's room will need to be different from a teenager's. But certain basic principles are fundamental to organizing any child's room. These strategies not only help with the room's physical setup, they also help train the occupant how to stay organized. Teach your children good organization habits in their own rooms, and they'll carry those habits to the rest of the house.

The key to helping children keep their rooms in order is the way you integrate storage and organization aids into the design of the room. Just putting a laundry hamper and toy box where kids can see them isn't going to do it.

The more the process of organizing—putting things away in the right place, picking up as you go, and so on—is innovative, interesting, and part of a daily routine, the more likely children will be to make the effort to stay organized. This can mean purchasing interesting storage solutions, thinking up novel approaches, and even letting kids come up with fun organizing and storage solutions as part of a creative exercise.

The storage solutions you pick should be as flexible as possible, and they should be safe. Because your child moves quickly through stages and ages, whatever you use as storage in a child's bedroom should be adaptable. For instance, using real wood chests that can be repainted and repurposed as your child ages is often a more economical option than a less expensive, molded-plastic, cartoon-character toy chest. The solutions suggested in this chapter are adaptable to a range of ages.

Although the zones presented here cover elements in most kids' rooms, one or more may not be applicable to your child's room. For instance, art and play areas may be one and the same in your son or

A toddler's room has a tall dresser with abundant storage and a high surface the child can't reach—or lay toys on. The toy chest has safety hinges and all-wood construction that ensures it can be redecorated and reused as the child grows.

daughter's room. So pick the zones that apply to your child and tackle them in an order that makes sense for you. Note that the times listed for each zone reflect an adult organizing the zone. If you are working through the process with a child, you'll naturally have to set aside more time. Start with the messiest area, and work from there. Including your child in the process and bringing in fun, creativity, and innovation may make straightening up your child's room easier on both of you.

This teen girl's room proves that a kid's room can be "hip" *and* orderly. The steel "locker" type pieces can be stripped and repainted for later use in a rec room, garage, or an adult's bedroom.

A good work-station provides a dedicated place for homework and room for a small computer setup. The keyboard sits on a platform that slides out of the way and the chair rolls under the desk, keeping the whole unit as contained as possible.

Combining storage with a handy place to sit while dressing, this unit is made more convenient with casters. The drawers can store folded clothes, jackets, blankets, or back issues of teen fashion magazines.

A simple dresser offers plenty of room for folded clothes and underwear. A nice set of decorative glass vases not only adds a stylish touch to the room, it also discourages the placement of loose clothing on the dresser.

Deep underbed storage provides a place for extra comforters or blankets, or for toys or collectibles the child wants, but does not play with anymore.

Toy Storage

30 MINUTES

Young kids love their toys. The presence of toys is one of the key elements that separates a child's bedroom from an adult's. Given the diversity of sizes and shapes, the amount of small, removable pieces, and frequency of use, it's no wonder that toys are the largest source of clutter in any young child's room.

The first step to getting toys in order is winnowing out broken toys, safety hazards, and those the child has outgrown. Try to do this with your child: you may be surprised what he or she no longer wants to keep.

The next step to organizing toys involves a lot more than just a bigger toy box. Infants, toddlers, and preteens present the biggest toy-management challenges.

➤ INFANTS: If you have an infant, you're in control of the toys. But that can become quite a chore because so many people give toys as gifts. Don't be afraid to donate toys that never get played with or are stored in closets. Create a "favorites" bag for the small toys that your child likes the most. You can use a backpack or any other fabric bag with a loop or handle (even a mesh laundry bag will work). Fill the bag with the baby's favorite toys and then put it on the floor next to the crib when your child is in the crib. The bag can move wherever the child goes—to the playpen, changing table, stroller, and beyond. That way, you'll always have a place for your child's favorite toys. Because infants make a mess of things within their reach, keep extra stuffed animals, learning toys, and toys for later ages together by type on a high shelf or in a box with a latch.

➤ TODDLERS TO PRETEENS: Beyond the age of two, children's toy collections become increasingly diverse and extensive.

A wire toy bin can keep loose toys or sports gear in order and in sight. Handy in the closet or out in the open, these types of organizers adapt easily to changing needs as the child grows.

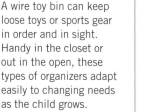

STORAGE IN STYLE

TOY POCKETS: Recycle an old art apron with clear pockets or a plastic hanging shoe bag as easy-to-reach containers for all those small toys. These are ideal for a variety of toys, from baby rattles to army men to Barbie accessories. Simply hang the apron or shoe bag by hooks (or over a door if it has hanging brackets) within the child's reach. As your kids grow, they can change what's kept in the pockets.

STORAGE IN STYLE

NET GAIN: Create a quick and easy toy catchall that will serve your child from infancy through the preteen years. Simply buy a mesh toy "net" that attaches in the corner of a wall. The net creates a hammock to hold soft toys such as stuffed animals. Or make your own toy net with three screw-in hooks and a mesh laundry bag or mesh child safety gate. Just place two of the hooks on perpendicular walls, and a third near where the walls meet in the corner. Then attach the netting like a hammock, allowing it to pouch in the middle.

Keeping the growing population of toys in line requires a variety of storage solutions.

Benches, boxes, and chests can provide ample storage to accommodate an assortment of toys. If you use a toy box, consider buying one without a lid or removing the lid from the one you have. That way the child sees exactly where the toys are supposed to go, and can literally throw them in there. It removes one step in the process—that of opening the lid—making it much easier to stay organized. It also removes the possibility of the lid closing on small fingers. If you keep the lid, look for boxes with finger cutouts and lid-control devices with safety hinges. Bench toy boxes serve two purposes: seating and storage. Find one with a slatted lid so it's easy to see the toys inside.

Bin consoles are great solutions for rooms with more than one child. These are essentially groups of stacked cubes with pullout baskets. The cubes can be self-standing or mounted on a wall—but it's always better to keep things low so small children can get to what they need without being tempted to climb. Toys in consoles can be segregated by type or by child. Some consoles come with simple transparent boxes that let the child see what's inside. Other units use wicker or wood baskets that can be labeled with words, a picture, or an icon (for example, twist-tying a small stuffed bunny to the front of a basket containing stuffed animals). Choose a stylish, well-made bin console and it will serve your child from the crib through college.

Shelves are ideal for board games, puzzles, and "collections" of toys. Dedicating a shelf to one type of toy ensures that your child is very clear about where that type of toy goes when not

Where space is at a premium or there are too many toys for the toy chest, look to the back of a door for help. This overdoor organizer keeps toys in their own pockets. This works well hung on the main door to the room, or hidden behind a hinged closet door.

THE INSIDE SCOOP

BAG IT: A great solution for all those bulky toy pieces, like lightweight building blocks, is large, clear plastic bags. Hang the bag by its handles from hooks or pegs in the closet, or from a row of hooks mounted high up on the wall. The bags keep the clutter off the floor, and the child can see through the bag to pick out what he or she wants to play with. Just make sure that the bags are placed well out of the reach of small children.

STORAGE IN STYLE

HANDY HAMPER: Woven fabric or wicker laundry hampers can serve as great toy keepers for bigger kids (the child needs to be able to reach to the bottom). They can be painted to suit the child's taste, and can be painted again later and used once more as a hamper when your child gets older.

being used. For instance, devote a shelf to action figures so your grade-school child knows where the figures are, and can take pride in keeping the toys in good shape. Board games and puzzles should be placed on shelves that leave plenty of room for new games. If the games are usually played with the entire family, move them to where there is more available space, such as a shelf in the family room.

➤ **TEENS:** Once into their teens, most kids leave the stuffed animals and power figures behind, opting for more high-tech forms of entertainment. Your child's room needs to reflect that change. Chances are your son or daughter listens to music and may well have a handheld electronic video game console. These high-tech and expensive items need a safe place to stay when they are not in use, so that they don't get lost or

A mix of toy storage options keeps any play space neat and orderly. This child's room includes a large toy chest, large standing shelves, and wall-mounted shelves. All can be repainted for use in just about any room in the house when the child gets older.

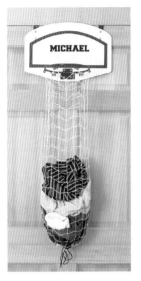

Novelty hampers provide amusement and a clutter solution. This one has hooks to hang conveniently on the back of the door. The basketball version encourages shooting until the clothes are "dunked."

Making storage apparent helps children see where things go. This inexpensive wire cube unit can be reconfigured to suit the child's storage needs and the space available. It can be freestanding or wall-mounted, and the cubes accommodate a range of items, from books to toys.

broken. If your teen's room includes a stereo, keep portable music players and handheld game consoles in a padded tray or box near it. It's best if this container has a drawer or enough extra space for batteries and any other peripherals such as the cord that connects the music player to a computer. If the room doesn't have a stereo, keep the box or tray near where your teen listens to the music player—a homework area or a bed. Let your son or daughter pick out a CD rack to organize his or her music collection.

ZONE 2

Work/Art Space

1 HOUR

Encourage your child's creativity by creating a real art area. You don't need a lot of space, just enough for a small desk or table, a light, a chair or bench, and a little spot for art supplies. This area can also function as a work area, where your child can do homework or school projects as he or she grows. Obviously, the space will need to expand as your child grows into his or her teen years. High school art and science projects tend to take up more room than homework assignments from earlier years. Preteens and teens will also use different equipment—most notably, computers.

➤ FURNITURE: The bedroom space will need to change as your child grows older, so you should choose furniture and organizers for their adaptability. If you decide to buy an easel for your child, you might want to go the extra expense for a wood unit, with telescoping legs, that can grow as your child does. Older kids can also make good use of an art area, but the furniture will need to change to accommodate their larger bodies. A few pieces, such as small, toddler-size chairs, will not make the transition. Other pieces require a little ingenuity to adapt over time. For instance, a secondhand drafting table can be lowered or raised to accommodate children of different ages. If you are hoping to use a piece such as a desk for the entire time the child lives at home, consider first how the desk will be used when the child is older (younger children require less space). A teen is likely to need space on a desk for a computer, a monitor, and—possibly—a phone.

A bin console provides easy, accessible storage for art supplies, clothes, toys, and more. Choose one with bins that pull out. The rugged plastic types here are durable and easy to clean, and the unit can work in the pantry, garage, or crafts room when your child outgrows it.

A self-contained art wardrobe is an ideal piece of furniture for the creative pre-teen. Offering plenty of room to work and store supplies, the desk can be folded down and out of the way—and the wardrobe closed—when not in use.

THE ART AREA RULES

1. Keep cleanup gear close. A supply of paper towels, moist towelettes, or rags makes it more likely that accidents will get cleaned up promptly.

2. Use appropriate supplies. Kids' art supplies should be non-toxic and water-soluble. Never adapt professional-quality paints or supplies for children's art projects.

3. Contain creativity. Store all art supplies in cleanable containers in the art area. Use recycled plastic containers for disposable purposes, such as mixing paints. Explain to kids the need to put away clay and put tops on paints to keep supplies fresh.

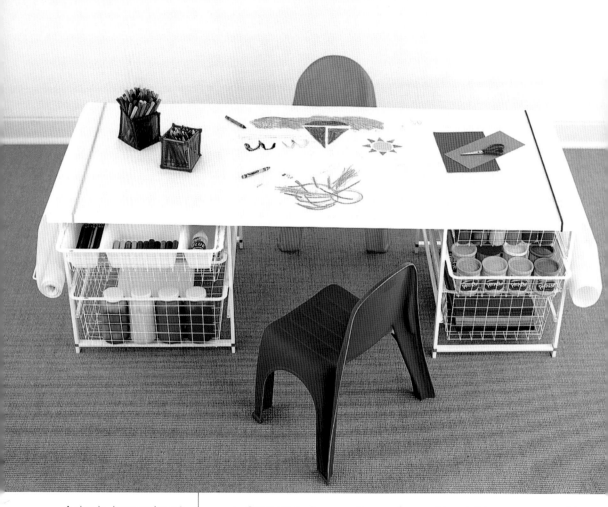

A simple, inexpensive art table for small children can supply hours of fun. This one includes storage bins as end supports and built-in rollers for rolls of art paper.

➤ **SUPPLIES:** Art supplies can be used by children young or old. Keep them organized and they are less likely to get lost, damaged, or destroyed. An all-in-one art kit is a good idea for any child, and you can make your own from drawer organizers arranged in a large, clear plastic box. Teen artists will need enough room to slide a full-sized art portfolio behind a desk or against a wall. As your teen begins to specialize in an art form, the supplies he or she buys will likely be self-contained, such as a case that holds sketching chalks.

➤ **ARTWORK:** Finished artwork, from finger paintings to clay sculptures, can become clutter. The way to organize finished artwork is to display it or store it.

Two-dimensional artworks, such as painted pictures and sketches, are easy to display. Pin them up on a corkboard or frame

THE INSIDE SCOOP

HIGH WIRE ACT: Use a thin cable (available at home centers), clothesline, or length of sturdy twine to make a gallery display of your child's sketches or paintings. String the cable or twine between two walls and hang the artwork with binder clips or clothespins. Make sure your child signs his or her pieces!

STORAGE IN STYLE

FANTASTIC PLASTIC: Recycle plastic containers with lids (like margarine tubs) and plastic jars or wide-mouthed plastic drink bottles for your children's art supplies. Bins and tubs can be used to keep individual jars of paint in order, and for other loose art supplies. Use taller containers for loose brushes, pencils, and crayons. Your child's first art project can be decorating these containers.

STUCK UP: For fun and flexible storage, it would be hard to beat a Velcro wall. Buy Velcro straps in packs at home centers or hardware stores (they come in regular and heavy duty varieties—buy the one rated for the weight of what you will be hanging). Each strip has a mate and an adhesive back. Stick a series of strips on the wall to hold fuzzy stuffed animals or larger toys to which you've attached a mating strip. You can even put a small piece of mating strip on the underside of jacket collars so kids can hang their jackets on the wall!

them with an inexpensive frame from an art store. Store these pieces in a three-hole binder (if they can be punched without damaging the image), an over-sized folder with pockets, a small hanging-file box, or an underbed plastic box. Or have your child draw or paint in an oversize art pad. Display the child's favorite piece by opening to that page and leaning the pad against the wall. After all the pages are used, store the pad on a shelf or in an underbed container with other treasured papers. Or you may opt to let the child decorate the entire room, to create his or her own gallery of artwork. As the child creates new artwork, you can rotate the work on display.

Three-dimensional art, such as papier-mâché masks or molded clay figures, should be displayed on high shelves, to prevent breakage. If you are storing three-dimensional art, use hard plastic or wood containers with straw or Styrofoam-peanut packing material to keep it safe.

Displaying kids' artwork is a sure way to keep it from becoming clutter. This simple solution involves just a length of strong string, pushpins, and a few decorative clips.

Below top: A traditional "Captain's" bed, with drawers as part of the base frame, can provide abundant extra storage in a child's room—and may even eliminate the need for a dresser.

Below bottom: An unusual bedside cabinet contains shelves instead of drawers—providing more accessibilty for the child and making it harder to misplace things.

ZONE 3

Bed/Play Area

1 HOUR

In a child's room, the bed and play area are usually all of one piece. Younger children incorporate the bed into their play, from using it as a stage for make-believe to creating a pillow-and-blanket fort. Older children, such as teens, continue to consider the bed an extension of their recreation area. They use it as a place to read, listen to music, and talk to their friends. The trick is to provide enough storage and organizers to keep things tidy around the bed without letting those additions become part of the problem.

Just as in adult bedrooms, a bedside table is essential. A good reading light connected to a remote switch (so you can make the lights go out when you need to) is a great feature of this area. And the bed itself not only offers play space, it also provides the same storage space that adult beds do. Lastly, a small play table can be an excellent addition to a larger room.

➤ **BEDSIDE TABLE:** There's only one person in the bed, so there should be only one bedside table (unless, of course, there are two children in the same room). Just as with an adult's bedside table, a child's needs to be easily reachable from the bed—neither too tall nor too short. But a child's nightstand should be more modest. There can be a shelf underneath the top of the nightstand, but don't include a drawer because it will invite a disorderly collection of loose objects. Also keep in mind that—children's motor skills being what they are—anything on top of the nightstand is liable to fall to the floor at one time or another. Consider using a clip-on lamp, or one with a plastic base. There should be room enough for a book or two, a lamp, an alarm clock, a phone in the teen years, and not much else. Because children so often put things down without thinking, limit surfaces on which they can just set things down.

➤ BED: A child's bed has less room underneath than an adult's, but there is still enough space for significant underbed storage. A rolling box or tray is ideal for board games, clothes that you are waiting for your child to grow into, collections of artwork, or other long- or medium-term storage (for more on underbed storage see page 51).

Whatever type you choose, commit to some sort of underbed storage. Otherwise, this space is likely to become cluttered with in-line skates, stuffed animals, and various papers. Underbed organizers send the message to kids that the space is not to be used as a place to hide things.

Bunk beds have their own requirements. Because the sleeping areas are stacked, only one child will have access to the nightstand, but the child on top of the bunk still needs the storage space of a nightstand. Put up a small shelf for books and toys. Hang a lamp on the ceiling or wall, within reach of a child lying on the top bunk. You can also use a hanging basket as a nightstand of sorts for the top bunk.

A sturdy play table gives kids a chance to spread out and also confines messes to one area.

THE INSIDE SCOOP

EASY ILLUMINATION: Young children should have a convenient light source for when they have to get up at night or when they want to read before sleeping. Night-lights can be too weak, and traditional lamps can be difficult for young children to turn on in the dark. Instead, consider using battery-operated "touch lights." These inexpensive round lights mount on a wall or other flat surface, and are turned off and on by simply touching the face. They come in a range of decorative face covers such as moons, stars, and other fun designs. These are an especially good option for children sleeping on the top bunk of a bunk bed. You can also buy more conventional lamps—both wall-mounted and desk lamps—with touch bases that children can turn on and off just by touching.

TENT CONTROL: Kids love a "fort" of any kind, and today's indoor play tents are understandably a big favorite. But the tent can quickly become a clutter zone like no other. Control what goes in and out of the tent with a "tent keeper" bag. Give your kids a small fabric bag (even an old purse or tote bag will do) and tell them that toys can only go through the tent door when carried in the tent keeper. If the keeper is inside the tent when kids want to play, they must bring it—and the toys that went in with it—out, before anything else can go into the tent.

➤ **PLAY TABLE:** If the room is large, a play table can go a long way toward keeping the whole area in order. The play table should be big enough for children to play a board game on, but not so large that it impedes traffic flow. The best play tables are about as high as a coffee table and have a safely hinged top with a compartment underneath. Remove the table when your children reach their teen years—teens won't use it and replacing the table will eliminate one more surface that can gather clutter.

➤ **TEEN DRESSING AREA:** As children age, they become more conscious of their grooming habits. This is especially true for teenage girls. At some point, your daughter may want to convert part of the play area into a space for a vanity. A small table with a mirror and room for a makeup kit will usually suffice. Make sure your teen has a box that will hold all her makeup and grooming supplies, so that these don't sit around loose, waiting to become clutter in other parts of the room.

A modest dresser is fine for young children. This small three-drawer unit holds the folded clothes of a young boy. The drawer can be repurposed as a nightstand. As he ages, the dresser can be repurposed as a nightstand.

Clothes, Closets, and Dressers

⚙ 1 HOUR

Children's wardrobes are much simpler than what you'll find in an adult's closet (teenage girls excepted), so they require different storage and organization tools. The closet is where this difference is most glaring. Not only do the clothes have to be accessible to the smaller stature of children, clothes in a child's closet are also going to be rotated in and out frequently as the child grows. The closet setup will also have to change radically when children grow into their teen years and pay much more attention to their wardrobes.

Dirty clothes present another challenge in a kid's room. Whether in the closet or out in the open, a child's laundry bag should be placed as close as possible to where he or she undresses. Try to make

THE KID'S CLOTHES RULES

1. **Organize low to high.** What children wear every day should be within reach. Use high shelves and hard-to-reach areas for long-term storage.

2. **Avoid the hanger.** Kids, even teenagers, find hangers a hassle. If you want to get them to keep their clothes organized, avoid the hanger as much as possible. Most of what kids wear can be hung on hooks or pegs, or folded and stored on shelves or in drawers.

3. **Spell it out.** Even young children can be trained to put away clothes where they belong, especially if you use a device such as pictures taped to the front of the shelf for children who can't read, and funky colored labels for those who can.

4. **Laundry entertainment.** Make putting dirty clothes in the hamper fun to ensure that kids get in the habit. For small children, make a large clown face out of cardboard, with a big hole in the mouth, and put the face over the hamper.

Pre-teen and teen girls require a place for makeup and other beauty supplies. A fold-out cabinet with mirrors keeps brushes and other grooming supplies in one area.

using the bag or hamper as fun and interesting as you can. Put a basketball hoop over the top of the opening, or mount a target on the wall above the laundry bag.

➤ **KID'S CLOSET:** There are two key principles behind designing a child's closet to promote organization and fight clutter. First, a child is not going to use the closet like an adult might; the focus needs to be on easy access and intuitive location. Second, the closet will have to change as the child changes. The most blatant example of this is a closet hanging rod. Look to eliminate hanging rods in your young child's closet. Even if he or she has dress clothes, those clothes are so small that they can easily be laid flat in a drawer or on a shelf. (Where you don't have a flat surface large enough for a child's dress clothes—such as a boy's jacket—you will need to hang them.) As your child matures into adolescence and through the teen years, he or she is going to need more hanging storage (although still not as much as you require).

The better choice for most children is a closet comprised of shelves and drawer units. If you're leery of giving up all hanging storage, buy wire shelves with a hanging bar incorporated into their construction. Organize shelves by type of clothing, using attached shelf dividers as necessary. This will make it clear to children what goes where, and give them a sense of how organization works. To keep apace of your child's changing stages as he or she grows, use closet shelves and drawer units with brackets that allow complete repositioning. Drawers used in a child's closet should be transparent plastic or wire mesh so the child can see what's inside. Use simple wood or wire-mesh units for shoes, and add extra units as the child's shoe collection grows.

➤ **THE DRESSER:** A dresser is the closet overflow in a child's room. Ideally, you should buy a three-drawer wooden changing table that can be used for your infant, and then converted to a dresser as your child becomes a toddler and then a teenager. For infants, use dividers to organize drawers by type of clothing or type of cleanup aids (wet wipes

Opposite: A teenage girl's closet reflects the need for stylish storage. Varied hanging storage holds dresses, skirts, and shirts, while a column of sleek mesh baskets keeps folded clothes and accessories in order. A set of plastic compartments turns two mesh bins into storage drawers for small loose items.

THE INSIDE SCOOP

HANG TWO: If you prefer to use a hanging bar for your young child's dress clothes, make sure the clothes are in the child's reach. Hang a bar from the existing closet rod. Simply tie two 6-foot lengths of clothesline or other nylon rope to form two loops around the existing rod. Then slide a rod made from a cut-down broomstick, round wooden stick, or pipe through the bottom of the loops.

With a little planning, an infant's closet can be arranged to hold almost all of the child's clothing, bedding, towels, and accessories.

and wash clothes in one section, one-piece underclothes in another). With toddlers, try to keep just one type of clothing per drawer. To help your toddler learn where clothes are, take a picture of a shirt or pair of pants and stick it to the front of the drawer that holds those clothes. Be sure to secure a child's dresser with safety straps to avoid accidental tip-over. In the teen years, help your child keep organized by using drawer dividers. The more logical you can be in organizing the clothes, the easier it will be for your son or daughter to find garments and get dressed without asking you repeatedly where his or her favorite T-shirt is. Make sure the drawer divisions reflect how your teen actually dresses. For instance, he likely uses T-shirts as undergarments, has other T-shirts to use as everyday outerwear, and has a third group for special occasions such as concerts. Each type should be in its own place in the dresser.

STORAGE IN STYLE

MAGAZINE BANK: Children love to collect issues of their favorite magazines. Keeping those loose-bound volumes from spreading all over is easier than it may appear. Either buy plastic magazine "library boxes," or make your own. Use an overnight delivery box or a cereal box, and with the box standing on its base, remove the top and cut one of the narrow sides of the box from top to midpoint, spine to spine. The opening will let kids see what issues are stored, and the box will keep them in order.

Book Storage

15 MINUTES

Children of any age can enjoy books. Reading to infants is a great
way to bond with young children, and toddlers can begin to learn
their alphabet by looking at board books. Older children can choose
what they want to read. But books need to be kept in good shape for
anyone to enjoy them.

That's why books should never be put into a toy box where the
spines are likely to get broken and the pages dislocated. A bookshelf is
an essential piece of furniture in any child's room.

A standing bookshelf is preferable to a wall-mounted shelf,
because children—even older children—tend to be careless in their
movements and a wall-mounted shelf may fall after being bumped
one time too many. Standing bookshelves represent adaptable space
in a kid's room: If you have more space than books, you can always
use the extra for storing boxes of baseball cards, dioramas, or the latest science project. Use a low, wide bookshelf to keep the books
within the child's reach and to discourage climbing. Always anchor
standing bookshelves to a wall with safety straps.

Special Storage

30 MINUTES

A few specialty products can help kids keep their lives organized
with a minimum of fuss and effort on their part. The key is to make
the process as fundamental and clear as possible.

A backpack hook seems an unlikely aid in a child's bedroom, but
it can help keep your child focused on his or her studies (and keep
the backpack clean and neat in the process). Attach a hook near the
door to the room. Before the child can hang the backpack on the

Shelving units should reflect the personality of the child and offer enough space for storing art projects, books, and necessities. Bins provide additional storage alternatives. In later years, these all-wood shelves can be refinished for duty in a family room or adult bedroom.

hook—where it's supposed to go—he or she has to empty the contents. This will prevent forgotten homework assignments that would otherwise be balled up at the bottom of the backpack. It also avoids the mess of a week-old, half-eaten sandwich or a rotten, squashed banana.

Hanging organizers are the best use of a closet rod—and they can be hung from the top of a door or the bottom of a wire shelf if you've removed the rod. These organizers are canvas columns of compartments that can be used to store a wide range of items, from clothes to shoes to stuffed toys. They are especially useful for helping kids keep clothing, school gear, and other important items straight. Label each compartment in the organizer with a day of the week. Small children can keep each day's clothes in the compartments so they're ready to go in the morning. Older kids can use the organizer to keep homework assignments straight, school projects in one place, and the right gear or musical instruments ready for the day they're needed.

KEEPING UP

Maintaining your child's room as a clutter-free environment is easy once you involve your child. He or she is never too young to learn the value of a neat living space, and there are many ways to get your child into the organizing habit.

• **Toy patrol:** Every night, as part of the bedtime ritual, your child should put toys back where they belong.

• **The pickup path:** If children—from young kids through teens—can't walk directly to their bed from the door, they need to pick up whatever is in their path and put it where it belongs.

• **Weekly visits:** Once a week, make sure the storage in your child's room is being used correctly. Are clothes being stuffed in the closet, and are dirty clothes thrown on the floor? Has your child's bedside table become a jumble of toys, bedtime books, and other loose items? Make a checklist of problem areas and give it to your child. Giving a child a checklist is much more effective than saying "clean your room," because checklists provide defined—rather than vague—goals. After a few checklists, most children (beyond the toddler years) learn to periodically do their own inspections.

CHAPTER 3

Bathrooms

The bathroom is one of the busiest spaces in the home, so it doesn't take long for this smallest of rooms to become overrun with wet towels, dirty clothes, makeup clutter, and half-empty shampoo bottles.

The battle to prevent all this clutter is made more challenging because of the confined dimensions of any bathroom. Even large bathrooms are limited in space, and clutter accumulates quickly. But you can actually use the space limitations to your advantage. It's fairly simple to organize and position necessities close to where they will be used, so they can easily be put back.

Introducing order to this hectic room is a matter of tailoring solutions to the number and type of people using the bathroom. (The number of people using the bathroom will also affect the time each zone takes to organize. The times listed take into account the needs of a family of four. If you're the only person using the bathroom, you can expect to cut those times in half.) In a woman's bathroom, the issue may be the need to find effective storage for cosmetics and personal care products. If one or more children are using the bathroom, it's important to establish a place for bath toys and dirty clothes. Men require some sort of organized station to deal with their daily shaving needs. And the general family bathroom faces all these challenges, plus organizational challenges like tissues, toilet paper, cups, medicine, towels, and more. But don't be discouraged; follow the zones in order, and you'll have more bathroom storage than you have ever thought possible, organized in a way that will make the space easier to use and keep clean.

Opposite: A busy family bathroom is well served by a vanity with a mix of cabinets and drawers. A towel tower with cubbies for rolled-up towels adds specialized storage.

THE INSIDE SCOOP

SMALLER IS BETTER: Limit the size of your bathroom wastebasket to keep things tidier. A smaller wastebasket gets emptied more often, and it's easier to notice if something has accidentally fallen into the trash. As in the kitchen, keep a few plastic trash bags (or old supermarket bags) at the bottom of the wastebasket to encourage easy and frequent disposal.

Medicine Cabinet

30 MINUTES

Almost every bathroom has one, because a medicine cabinet is an amazingly useful feature. It's the ideal place to keep all those small everyday items used in the bathroom—from toothpaste to eye drops to prescription medicines (stored according to manufacturers' instructions)—well organized and out of view.

But precisely because the storage is hidden and handy, a medicine cabinet tends to become the "junk drawer" of the bathroom. For whatever reason, we are often reluctant to remove anything from the medicine cabinet, allowing it to fill to capacity with empty cosmetic bottles, used, rolled-up toothpaste tubes, and useless, out-of-date medicines.

That's why the first step in any bathroom organization effort is to remove everything in the medicine cabinet and give the cabinet a good cleaning. Now look at what you've removed and throw away empty containers. Properly discard old medicines that are past their expiration dates. (Check with your local poison control center for their recommendations on how to discard expired medicines.) This includes both over-the-counter aids such as aspirin and indigestion remedies, and prescription medicines. Be aware that even herbal remedies and "natural" products such as melatonin carry expiration dates. Remember, too, that all medicine cabinets and drawers should be equipped with a safety locking device.

Opposite: In a bathroom without a medicine cabinet, other types of concealed storage must replace the lost space. This simple pedestal sink has a wraparound cabinet with a twist lock that can safely hold all the items that would have been kept in the medicine cabinet.

THE INSIDE SCOOP

BUILT-ON OPTION: Some bathrooms are equipped with a wall-mounted mirror instead of a built-in medicine cabinet. But that doesn't mean you have to do without the handy storage a cabinet provides. Surface-mounted cabinets are simply attached right to the wall over the sink. Although these are shallower than built-in units, they still provide a wealth of accessible storage and only take about 30 minutes to install. You'll find an excellent selection at large home centers.

Now organize what's left by use. For instance, put everything having to do with dental care (floss, toothpaste, mouthwash) in one area of the medicine cabinet. In some cases, what you would normally want to put in the cabinet won't fit. An economy-size bottle of mouthwash may be too big to stand upright, so you'll need to store it elsewhere. Find a smaller bottle or glass flask with a tight-fitting top, fill it with the mouthwash, and keep it in the cabinet. If you have limited sink-top space and no nearby shelves, you may want to keep your brush in the cabinet as well.

Sinks and Vanities

⚙ 1 HOUR

The area around your sink provides a place to put everyday items near where they will be used. The vanity that holds the sink often includes abundant storage for the many things that wouldn't fit into a cabinet or even on a shelf. If you're thinking of installing a vanity, the customized storage options are amazingly diverse. Even if you're working with an existing unit, you can adapt it for a multitude of specialized storage needs.

Make the most of a sink and vanity area by storing supplies where their size and shape fit best. For instance, if you have a shelf in the vanity on the side nearest the toilet, store extra rolls of toilet paper there. But you'll need to figure out how many rolls will fill the shelf, because buying more than this will mean cluttering up another space with the extra rolls.

Organize this zone from top to bottom, working from the sink top down to the drawers, if the vanity has them, and finishing

Below left: An attractive sink-top carryall keeps canisters and loose items under control and can be moved to wherever is most convenient.

Below right: Beating clutter on the sink top means keeping all loose items contained, and this unit does the job by corralling toothbrushes, hand soap, and a rinse cup in one handy unit.

with the undersink cabinet space. Whatever you keep on the sink top should be kept in one of the storage options outlined below, in order to keep clutter in check. The same is true of the undersink space; choose storage options that serve your needs, but make sure everything you store is contained in some way.

Keep in mind that any door or drawer a young child can reach needs a safety latch. This is especially important for the undersink area, where caustic cleaners are often kept.

➤ **TOP SURFACE:** This is where you keep personal care supplies and equipment you use every day, as well as decorative toiletries. Whatever you put on the surface should be contained. For instance, rather than laying your toothbrush next to a cup, use a toothbrush-holder set with a matching rinse cup. Better yet, use a simple toothbrush holder and add a paper-cup dispenser to your sink top or wall. The improved hygiene will be well worth the extra cost. Cosmetics are commonly placed on the vanity surface, but limit these to the makeup you use everyday. Other cosmetics should be stored in a drawer. You can also use a cosmetics carousel or vanity valet to organize your makeup in style. If you don't want to spend the money, keep your makeup corralled in a basket, decorative bowl, or a stylish plastic zip bag. Men's shaving products are preferably kept in the medicine cabinet, although, depending on the space available, you can keep them on the sink top in a razor-and-shaving-cream caddy. You'll want to keep hand soap near the sink, but use liquid soap in a dispenser. Bar soap, even when it's in a soap dish, tends to get messy quickly. Many people also like to keep their hair dryer and hair-grooming tools out and ready to use. If you keep these on top of the vanity, put them in a hair-care organizer that will hold the dryer, brushes, and combs in their own compartments. Organize hair care products in a separate tray or bin.

➤ **DRAWERS:** Vanity drawers can be handy to store some of what might otherwise clutter the surface. In fact, drawers represent an

THE INSIDE SCOOP

COSMETIC AGING: Makeup has a life span, and you should only store cosmetics that are safe and usable. As a general rule, keep everything as tightly sealed and free of contaminants as possible to extend the life of the product. Throw away makeup if you notice odor, color, or texture changes. Here are time-frames after which you should discard makeup:

Mascara	3 months
Eye	3 months
Foundation and concealer	6 to 8 months
Nail polish	2 years
Lipstick	Up to 3 years
Compact powder	Up to 3 years
Face/cheek	Up to 3 years

opportunity to organize often-used supplies such as cosmetics, while still providing quick and easy access. Today's custom vanities also provide more drawer options, including large and deep drawers in place of shelves. How you organize your drawers is going to depend in large part on what you need to store in them.

Jewelry might find its way into your bathroom if you accessorize as the final phase of applying makeup. If you put your jewelry on in the bathroom, you should have a drawer dedicated to keeping it in order. Use preformed plastic or wooden jewelry inserts to keep everything tidy, or go with a more inexpensive option such as muffin trays or rows of votive candleholders. Each different type of jewelry should have its own container. Just be sure to keep your jewelry away from water, which can cause corrosion, rust, or discoloration of jewelry.

Makeup is easily organized in drawers. First, go through all your makeup and throw out anything that has expired (see box above). Then create a makeup organizer. Because of the variety of shapes and sizes, custom plastic compartments that snap together are excellent for keeping cosmetics in order. You can also adapt a flatware caddy to hold makeup brushes, bottles of nail polish, and other beauty aids.

Towels and washcloths can be stored in the custom drawers of larger vanities. Special tilt-down drawers provide plenty of space for folded or rolled towels, or even a bathrobe.

➤ UNDERSINK AREA: This can be an awkward storage space given the presence of pipes, but the height and depth make it useful for storing many larger bathroom items—from personal care products to cleaning tools to a large amount of backup supplies. The undersink area is also a good place to conceal those things you don't want to leave out in the open, such as a toilet brush, a plunger, and some personal care products. The best way to turn the space into effective storage is to use some sort of divider, such as shelves or stacking bins. Organized properly, the undersink area can become the pantry of the bathroom. But without storage containers, it will become a messy, cluttered area.

Door racks can be mounted on the inside of vanity cabinet doors to hold magazines and packaged personal care products. These are available as simple plastic grids that form pockets for flat items, or more complex wire structures with separate storage compartments to hold different shapes and sizes.

Baskets and specialized buckets keep bathroom cleaning supplies collected in one place. You can choose from simple plastic mesh baskets or go with more complex buckets, with handles and compartments for different types of cleaning supplies. If you have a lot of supplies or equipment to store, buy a sliding rack. The best have multiple tiers of adjustable storage and sit on smooth, gliding runners that provide the ultimate in access to undersink storage.

Undersink shelves can be sized and positioned to suit the space and most are adjustable. Special shelving units clamp onto and hang

Below left: Slide-out bins make the most of under-sink space, providing a place for toiletries and bathroom supplies. This unit is freestanding, so it doesn't require any installation.

Below right: Optimize a vanity with small organiz-ers that provide storage for specific items and make the most of open undersink space. This handy rack is hung from the inside of the vanity door and keeps a curling iron, hairdryer, and hair care products in one easy-to-reach place.

Built-in undersink shelves are another excellent way to organize a space that is often left unused or in disorder.

from the pipes, for efficient use of the space. Choose shelves based on what needs to go under the sink. For towels, you can use wider, inexpensive wire-grid shelves. For heavier supplies such as bottles of rubbing alcohol, mouthwash, and other personal care products, use sturdy, bin-type shelves.

ZONE 3

Shower and Bath

🕐 30 MINUTES

Although the shower stall and bathtub have little existing storage space, it's easy to beat clutter in this area with just a few innovative organization aids. Since everyone in the house probably takes a shower or bath daily, putting soap and bathing supplies within easy reach will automatically reduce clutter and frustration.

➤ **BATHING AND HAIR-CARE PRODUCTS:** Organize these everyday essentials in a wire or plastic storage container; otherwise, they will just clutter up the edges of the tub or shower surround. Use one that can comfortably hold all the hair-care products you and others in your household use, along with a loofah, a washcloth, and any other personal care products you use in the shower (which may include shaving supplies for both men and women). Pick a smaller two- or three-shelf container if your needs are modest. You can select models that attach directly to the tile, either with special mounting hardware or with suction cups. Or, for a simpler option, turn to caddies with hooks that hang from the showerhead stem. Make sure you buy one with the features that match the way you shower. If you use bar soap, you'll need a unit with a soap dish. If many people use the shower, you'll probably be better served by wide corner baskets on a tension pole. The pole is secured between the ceiling and the tub lip, and usually comes with three or four triangular basket shelves. Some even include a suspended no-fog mirror for shaving in the shower.

Organizers such as these keep all your shower supplies in one place. The shower-neck hanging rack keeps shampoo and other personal care products out of the way, but within reach. The suction cup holder can be stuck anywhere that is convenient within the shower. Both have ample compartments for different size bottles and hooks for utensils such as scrub brushes and razors.

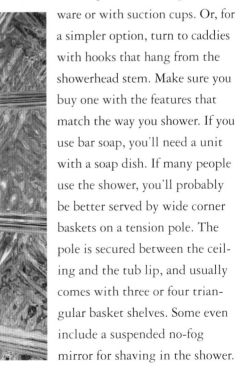

Kids are more likely to use organizers that inspire their sense of fun, making this mesh toy bag a winner in the tub. The suction-cup attachments allow you to place it at the child's level during bathing, ensuring that toys get put back at the end of bath time.

If you regularly use a washcloth, be sure any shelving units you buy have a hook, or buy a separate suction-cup hook.

➤ TOYS: Children's bath toys are essential to happy bath times, but if left unrestrained they can become slippery hazards underfoot, not to mention irksome floor clutter. It's a simple matter to keep them contained. Just pick an organizer that is large enough for all the toys (and then some) and one that can survive being waterlogged. The container can be a plastic bucket or bin, but needs to have holes in it so toys can drain after play. Keep it on a mat under the sink. Or, if you don't mind having the toys around at all times, keep them in a mesh shower-toy bag with suction-cup mounts. These range in style from simple net bags to elaborate cartoon-character organizers. The advantage of these types of toy holders is that you can rinse the toys off in the holder after play, and then just hang it up to dry on the wall. You can also buy hanging organizers that drape over the lip of the tub and can be hung elsewhere to dry out after bath time. These are great for holding toys, children's shampoo, and grooming aids such as brushes.

STORAGE IN STYLE

POCKET PURPOSE: Store children's bath toys in an innovative way: Use novelty "pocket" shower curtains positioned inside out. With the pockets on the shower side, the toys are easy to reach and create a fun look. Punch small holes in the pockets if they don't already have them, so water can drain.

THE INSIDE SCOOP

DISPENSING WISDOM: If many people use the shower, you might consider a hotel-style dispenser for liquid body wash, shampoo, and conditioner. These types of dispensers make showering easier and keep the shower and tub area more orderly. Choose from a single molded unit with three refillable chambers, or three decorative, matching bottle dispensers grouped in a single bracket.

STRONG ATTRACTION: Adhesive magnetic strips or screw-on magnetic plates are a great way to store metal objects used every day, like a metal-handled gum massager, nail clippers, or tweezers. Buy strips or other magnetic fasteners at home centers or hardware stores, and mount them on the wall over the sink or vanity, or wherever you do your personal grooming.

Toilet Storage

🕐 1 HOUR

A cramped bathroom requires that you look to the area around the toilet for storage. Although this may seem an unlikely region, you'll find a diversity of storage containers designed to take advantage of the odd spaces around a toilet. To start with, the toilet tank provides an accessible, flat surface. The thin gaps between toilet and vanity or toilet and tub are also adaptable for storage. The wall above the toilet is fair game as well. To truly defeat bathroom clutter, carefully assess how much storage you need in addition to what is already available in the medicine cabinet, sink, and undersink areas. You should buy an all-in-one solution such as an étagère (see page 97) only if you can use all the storage—otherwise the open space will become an invitation for clutter.

➤ TANK TOP: You may have thought that the tank top was useful only to hold a box of tissues or an extra roll of toilet paper. Think again. You can purchase a well-designed "tank-top caddy" to hold a number of small items that might otherwise clutter the sink top. These organizers are especially useful if you have a pedestal sink with little or no surface to store the basics, such as nail clippers and other small grooming aids. You can also employ hanging tank bags, small fabric caddies that are draped over the top of the tank like saddlebags. These are best used for magazines but can also hold personal care supplies.

➤ SIDE STORAGE: In the bathroom, it's important to look everywhere for additional storage, including the slim spaces between the vanity cabinet and toilet, and toilet and bathtub. Manufacturers look to optimize these areas with storage containers ranging from the simple to the complex. A basic magazine rack will fit, for example. Many organizers are more specialized. If you have no other place to keep extra rolls of toilet paper, you can use a tissue stand or a more complex toilet-paper-roll dispenser. These range from basic chrome poles over which extra rolls are placed to sleek vertical columns that conceal the toilet paper, dispensing one roll at a time. Other less attractive bathroom equipment, such as toilet brushes and plungers, can be completely concealed next to the toilet in handsome chrome or colorful plastic holders. For smaller goods and varied supplies, you can use a thin "trolley" organizer, which is essentially a set of skinny drawers on wheels. These units roll right into the space next to a toilet.

➤ ÉTAGÈRES AND SHELVING: Before you choose between an étagère or shelves, decide how much extra storage space you need, and whether you would prefer exposed or hidden storage. Étagères—also sold as "space savers"—are essentially one-piece cabinet or shelving units, with extra long legs to stand on either side of the toilet tank. These units offer more storage than shelving does, and give you the option of using cabinets, shelves, or a combination of the two. Select from a remarkable diversity of styles including chrome, wood, wicker, plastic, and combinations of these with glass shelves and cabinets. All bathroom étagères are built to allow clearance for a person to sit down or get up from the toilet. The same is not true of all shelving. Be sure to buy shelving made specifically for the bathroom, or measure to prevent buying shelving that sticks too far out. Some of the best shelves for bathrooms are glass, because the material isn't harmed by the vast changes in heat and moisture to which a bathroom is regularly subjected. You can opt for coated-wire shelves, but they are far less attractive and small objects tend to fall through. Finished wood shelves and plastic are two other reasonable options.

ZONE 5

Walls, Doors, and Floor Space

⬤ 1 HOUR

Finding the maximum amount of storage in the bathroom requires looking at all surfaces as potential storage areas. In a bathroom with ample square footage, you'll want to use a portion of the floor for additional freestanding storage. In more compact bathrooms, extra storage can find a home on the walls or even the back of the door.

Some of the wall-hung storage options, such as towel bars, are common to most bathrooms. Other hanging storage units are more specialized and can be handy places for the overflow from under the sink and other areas of the bathroom.

Above left: A hard-working shelf unit provides plenty of open storage, a towel bar, and cubbies that segregate useful decorative containers. The wood construction can be painted or refinished to to suit the bathroom.

Above right: A freestanding heated towel rack provides luxury to go, with lots of room for extra towels. Move the rack out of the way for easy cleaning, or to have nice warm towels exactly where you want them.

➤ TOWEL STORAGE: Although this seems fairly straightforward, options for towel storage are wildly varied. Alternatives to a simple straight towel bar abound. Pick a multitier towel bar for a bathroom used by a large family. Choose a towel ring for smaller hand towels and where wall space is at a premium. Combine storage types by installing a towel-bar-and-shelf combination. If you live in a part of the country that experiences cold winters, look for heated towel racks so that you can step out of the shower and wrap yourself in a toasty towel. Of course, towels don't always have to be hung up. Sometimes, rolling them into tight tubes and stacking them on a shelf can be a way to store more towels in a small space. Rolled up towels can be stored in unconventional containers as well, such as wall-mounted terra-cotta planters. You should put up hooks or pegs for used towels to dry on. Folded towels can be stored on just about any flat surface, including a cabinet top or a wide shelf. Stack towels with the folded side out to make it easier to remove the one you want. If you have abundant floor space, you can even treat yourself to a standing towel-and-robe valet.

➤ MOUNTED CABINETS AND SHELVES: To display or not to display? That's the main question you need to answer when deciding between wall-mounted cabinets or shelves. With the range of prod-

Above left: In cramped quarters, the back of the bathroom door can provide a great place to hang towels for drying or easy access. A special overdoor hook set serves the purpose nicely.

Above right: Where space is not an issue, an independent standing cabinet can give you the extra storage you need exactly where you want it. The right cabinet can also add a stylish accent to the bathroom.

ucts available, you'll find a shelf or cabinet to fit in just about any space you might have. The one other factor that may affect your selection is door swing. If the bathroom is especially narrow, you'll want to limit your options to shelves or cabinets with sliding doors. Always measure the maximum dimensions of what you want to store before buying a cabinet.

➤ STANDING CABINETS AND STORAGE TOWERS: The range of available self-standing storage is every bit as varied as anything you can put on the wall. Buy a standing cabinet with glass fronts, or a storage tower with exposed shelves, if what you want to store is visually appealing. If you need a place for bottles of rubbing alcohol and other first-aid supplies, buy a unit with enclosed compartments or frosted-glass doors. Choose a tower or cabinet based on the amount of surface space you have—tall and skinny towers are best for a bathroom with cramped floor space. Short, broad cabinets are more effective in larger bathrooms. Choose a material based on your decorative style. You can select wood cabinets for a traditional look, or go for a sleeker look with a metal-and-glass tower. Bathrooms used by a lot of children may call for more durable furniture, such as plastic towers or cabinets. If you want to include a tower in a high-use bathroom, pick a pyramid style, which is less likely to tip over.

A wheeled bathroom trolley can provide some of the most versatile storage you can buy. The bins can be used for everything from hair care products to extra towels, and the mobility of these units let you position them right where you want them.

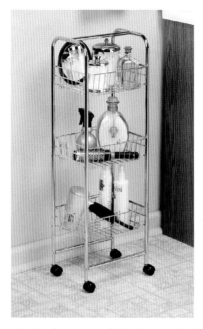

Always make sure any standing cabinet or storage tower is safely secured to the wall.

➤ **DOOR BACK:** In the search for extra storage in the bathroom, the door back has become every bit as viable as a wall. Manufacturers offer hanging towel racks and hooks, overdoor shelves, and small cabinets. As long as an organizer doesn't interfere with door swing, you can consider it for extra storage.

➤ **HAMPERS:** The bathroom is a convenient location for a clothes hamper, which in turn helps keep dirty clothes off the bathroom floor. Hampers range from the stylistically simple, such as the steel-tube frame with hanging fabric bag, to the more upscale wicker basket with canvas liner. If space is a concern, you can always use a laundry bag hung on the back of a door with a hook. If space is not an issue, you can keep dirty clothes organized and ready to go right into the wash by using a three-compartment hamper with individual bags for whites, bright colors, and darks.

KEEPING UP

Even though the bathroom is one of the most used spaces in the house, it requires minimal organization maintenance to keep the room free of clutter. Make maintenance a part of your regular cleaning.

• **Date check:** Every 6 months, go through the medicine cabinet and discard medications—both prescription and over-the-counter—that are past their expiration date.

• **Prune publications:** Every time you clean the bathroom, take a minute to look through any magazines in a magazine rack and remove old issues.

• **Inventory assessment:** On a monthly basis, before going shopping, check the levels of shampoo, conditioner, bath salts, and other products in the bathroom to see what needs to be replaced. Also check the number of toilet paper rolls you have in stock.

CHAPTER 4 | Family and Living Rooms

Traditionally, the family room was the informal center of relaxation and recreation for the family, while the living room served as the formal setting for entertaining and socializing. These days the roles usually blend between the two rooms. Many modern and contemporary homes simply don't have both rooms, or one has been put to another use, such as a home office. In any case, the line between formal entertaining and casual recreation has blurred. Friends today are just as likely to join in traditional "family fare," such as watching a movie together, as to be formally entertained in a prim and proper parlor. Even if your home has two distinct rooms, they are probably both used for living, relaxing, socializing, and entertaining.

Whether two rooms or one, the space presents complex organizational challenges. These rooms fulfill multiple roles, from home theater to party place to family conference center. Each of these roles calls for different types of organization and clutter-busting strategies, especially if you want a permanently clutter-free space.

Although the times given for each zone are fairly standard, your times will be shorter if you have minimal furniture, do little socializing, or aren't a big fan of video or audio entertainment.

You'll start with the zone that sees the most use and then proceed to less frequently used areas. So you'll start where movies and TV are watched, working to peripheral areas of relaxation. As you go along, you'll incorporate solutions to the clutter created by the different functions of the room, including relaxing, socializing, and entertaining.

Opposite: A cozy living room incorporates an ottoman as coffee table and a small reading table large enough to fit only a book. Every piece of furniture has a purpose, and the room is virtually clutter-free because of this.

Electronics

1 HOUR

You may not have the latest huge flat screen TV or a fancy, multi-speaker audio system, but chances are your electronics are the heart of your family or living room. The collection of media and equipment—whether grand or modest—is usually anchored by the TV. But in today's world, you likely have an increasing number of peripheral devices that work with the TV, including the cable or satellite box, a DVD and/or video player, a video game system, the home stereo system, and the family's computer.

Add to all these devices the cords, cables, and bits and pieces that naturally go with them—CDs, DVDs, remote controls, video games—and the potential for massive clutter is obvious. All this

This looks like a period piece, but is actually a stylized entertainment center with slots for all the stereo components, TV, and accessories. The unit includes pull-out doors to cover the electronics when not in use.

An antique cabinet serves as a signature piece in this eclectic living room, and has been adapted for use as an entertainment center, keeping the TV and DVD player hidden away when not in use.

equipment often starts out disorganized, because we buy it with little thought about how it will fit into the available space. That's why TVs often wind up on unsafe, rickety side tables or inexpensive TV stands that leave little room for other components. Bringing order to this often chaotic area will go a long way toward keeping the whole room tidy, and will make watching TV and listening to music much more enjoyable.

Start by looking at the equipment and media you own now, and think about what you are likely to add in the short term. Then it's just a matter of measuring and matching to find the furniture and solutions to contain your entertainment gear and keep the room neat.

➤ ENTERTAINMENT CENTER: A key piece of furniture for organizing electronic media, an entertainment center must adequately meet your needs if it is to prevent clutter. The right entertainment center can range from a modest television stand to a wall-filling, adjustable shelf system with custom conduits for cords and wires. You'll find a mind-boggling array of options in stores, or you may decide to adapt an existing piece of furniture (as long as it is stable and durable). Either way, the first step in finding the right entertainment center is to measure your electronics—depth, width, and height. Next, figure out what you want to store in the media center and what you don't see (the Entertainment Center Questions, page 105). This should give you a good sense of how much and what type of storage space you need, which will lead you to the right choice of entertainment center.

Adapted centers can be almost any large standing cabinet or shelf unit—from an old armoire to an unused dining-room hutch—that is not specifically designed as an entertainment center. If all

This stable and low-key TV cabinet provides a sturdy base for a wide, flat-screen TV, and ample room for all the video components associated with a home theater. Separate speakers are supported on matching stands.

you're looking to do is stack a couple of components underneath the TV, a sturdy table with a lower shelf may fill the bill. The main requirement is that the piece be deep enough to center your TV, with a shelf or support strong enough to hold the weight. Adapted entertainment centers should comfortably hold the electronics that work with the TV, an attached back must allow for holes through which cords can be run, and the center must permit proper component spacing and air circulation to cool the equipment. If you're storing a music or video collection— CDs, DVDs, and tapes—you'll need room either inside the unit or someplace on the outside for hanging storage. The one common drawback to adapted entertainment centers is TV positioning. Unless you're willing to do quite a bit of work, there is rarely a way to slide out the TV or swivel it side to side. This makes the TV harder to view if your seating surrounds the entertainment center in the standard horseshoe arrangement.

Store-bought stands and racks are excellent choices if you simply want someplace to put your TV, cable box, DVD player, and VCR. Stands and racks are sold by the size of the TV, and are available with fixed legs or casters. They come tall or wide, in a selection of design styles. If you are choosing a TV stand, you'll also want to look at containers for storing DVDs, videos, and CDs if you have them. Don't put TVs on a wall-mounted shelf. Not only are regular cathode-ray TVs too heavy for shelves, they have an off-center balance that makes them prone to tipping when they are not properly supported. Flat-screen TVs are also prone to tipping, but they can be mounted to the wall with special hardware.

Complete entertainment centers are a better choice if you want to store your stereo with your TV and include other components such as a video game console. Entertainment centers are limited

ENTERTAINMENT CENTER QUESTIONS

Given the dizzying array of entertainment center options, it's important to figure out exactly what you need in a unit. The answers to these questions will eliminate some options, and give you guidance on choosing among others.

How many components do you want to include in your entertainment center? Determine the basic number of shelves or compartments by how much equipment you need to store. Keep in mind that most electronics should have a little room around them for proper air circulation, which helps keep the electronics cool.

How many CDs do you own, and how many do you buy in a year? Unless you plan to purchase additional CD racks or other media storage containers, measure how much space your CD collection takes up and look for a unit with more space than necessary to account for music you'll buy in the near future.

How many DVDs do you own, and how many will be added to your collection? This will also affect how much shelving or other type of disk storage you need. DVDs are regularly sold in larger packages than the jewel cases that house CDs. This means DVDs usually can't be stored on the same shelf with CDs, unless you're willing to lay them on their sides.

Do you watch VHS tapes? How many do you own? You'll have to think carefully about this. If you have a DVD player, chances are you'll eventually replace your videotapes with DVD versions of the movies. If you're willing to do that now, you don't have to worry about storing something you'll eventually get rid of.

Will the stereo be stored with the TV? It is often easiest to combine all the electronics in one place.

Is the stereo going to be part of a home theater system? If so, what types of extra cables or hardware will you need to make that happen? If you have older electronics, you may not be able to run the TV through the stereo. Regardless, if you are keeping the stereo in the same place as the TV, the entertainment center should have space for the speakers, or a place where speaker mounts can be attached. This isn't an issue if the speakers are stand-alone, or if you are planning to put them on wall-mounted brackets away from the central entertainment center.

Do you prefer to keep electronics hidden? Or does a sleek, high-tech appearance suit your tastes? This is a big decision. The basic difference between entertainment systems is whether the storage is concealed or apparent. In most cases, a unit comprised of shelves will cost less than one with doors, drawers, sliding panels, or other concealed spaces.

How much wall space and floor space is available for the entertainment center? The answer to this question will determine whether you buy a tall and thin or a wide and low unit. If there is a lot of traffic flow around the front of the unit, use shelves instead of cabinets or choose doors that slide rather than open out.

Will you need to make connections to family members' computers or other devices, such as camcorders or projectors? If you will, you'll need access to the home components that will connect to these things, and possibly a place for the additional electronic devices.

only by the available space and your budget. Manufacturers offer these units in wood, glass, steel, and combinations, with adjustable shelves, cabinets to hide components, integrated media storage for disks and games, and other handy extras. They come sleek and high tech, or conservative and traditional. Some have a central pedestal supporting columns of shelves, while others are constructed like built-in bookshelves. Narrow your search by considering which entertainment centers provide the right amount of storage and fit into the space you have available. Then decide on a style that is in keeping with your tastes. As a rule of thumb, always look for slightly more shelf space than you need: Shelf space rarely goes to waste in the living or family room.

➤ SEPARATE STEREO: Sometimes it makes more sense to keep the stereo separate from the TV. The acoustics may be better in a different part of the room. Perhaps the electrical outlet near the TV can handle only the TV and video components. Or maybe you just prefer to listen to music in a different part of the house. Whatever the reason, a separate listening area should have room for all the parts of your stereo (the amplifier, tuner, receiver, CD player, and so on), and the storage containers you'll use for all your music. Mini or shelf stereo systems can simply be placed on a sturdy shelf. Component stereo systems—those in which the amplifier, tuner, receiver, and CD player are separate units—require a more complex storage structure. Stereo racks come with adjustable shelves and many have doors and adjustable clips or special channels for cables and wires. Use speaker stands to keep speakers off the floor (vibration through a floor can diminish sound quality) or mount them on walls with speaker brackets.

➤ VIDEO GAME SYSTEMS: The new generation of video game consoles do more than just play games. Most also function as DVD players, and low prices make them attractive even if you

THE INSIDE SCOOP

CONVERTING MEMORIES: You may be reluctant to part with VHS tapes you've shot. But you can reduce clutter and preserve precious images for decades to come by transferring home movies to DVD format. DVDs take up less room than videotapes and, if properly recorded and cared for, don't physically deteriorate as quickly as tapes do. The conversion process is relatively inexpensive. Contact your local photo lab or camera store. If you have a large number of tapes to convert, you might consider a home conversion unit that allows you to transfer images yourself.

A complete prefabricated entertainment center (at right) boasts special brackets for a large flat-panel TV, separate home-theater speaker stands, compartments for stereo and video components, and storage for CDs and DVDs.

use them only for that purpose. Depending on your TV, you may need to run the cables from the game box through an "RF modulator," a device that makes the signal playable on the TV. This unit is only about the size of a paperback book, but you need to make space for it. You'll also need to find a place for the video games themselves. Some look like DVDs and can be stored with CDs or DVDs. Others have different shapes. Manufacturers offer special cases and containers for these games—which are great options because the child can move the entire set of games instead of just one or two—but it's often cheaper and easier to just set aside a

portion of shelf space or drawer space near the game unit. The controllers require their own storage. If you have enough space in the entertainment center, they can simply be slid in alongside the game console. If space is tight, buy brackets to hold the controllers on the side or front of the entertainment center. Find appropriate brackets at large home centers. When the controllers have a place to go, they are less likely to be strewn about the floor, causing problems underfoot.

➤ CDS, DVDS, AND VIDEOS: Music and movie collections can quickly build to a substantial number of CDs or DVDs. You may also have a significant collection of older movies on videotape. Stored in loose piles, these become the worst kind of clutter. You need to organize your media to keep it from taking over the room, and so you can quickly find the movie or music you want. Many entertainment centers include shelves specially designed to store the unusual dimensions of

STORAGE IN STYLE

BINDERS, KEEPERS: CD and DVD collections can grow surprisingly large in a short time. It's not uncommon for an avid music listener to have a hundred or more CDs. In a house full of listeners, that number can grow almost exponentially. All those jewel cases will take up a vast amount of shelf space. But you don't have to be a prisoner to the jewel case. You can store your entire CD collection in a small, well-organized space by using a CD/DVD binder. These range from functional canvas or fabric types to sleek leather or funky colored versions. All come with pages that have pockets for the CDs or DVDs, with enough room for liner notes or box covers, and they all zip up to keep dust away from your disks.

jewel and DVD cases. You can also buy custom boxes designed to hold CDs, DVDs, or videotapes, and store the boxes on available shelf space. Often, though, there is no built-in capacity to efficiently store movies and music. In this case, you need to use special racks or holders for your loose media. There are two basic types of holders: standing and wall-mounted. If you want to store CDs, DVDs, and videotapes in the same rack, look for one with adjustable shelves. Swivel console towers offer abundant storage in a small space with excellent accessibility, and these are available to hold CDs or videotapes. You can choose from small spinning units that fit on top of the entertainment center or on a shelf, or larger units that stand on their own near the stereo or TV. Other types of tower racks and wall-mounted shelves are straightforward designs, available in wood, metal, glass, and plastic. Select according to budget, personal design taste, and the amount of storage you need. The key is to keep the storage as close as possible to where the CDs or DVDs will be played, so that they are more likely to get put back after use.

➤ VINYL RECORDS AND CASSETTE TAPES: If you've been collecting music for a long time, chances are you may still have cassette tapes and even older vinyl records. Keep your cassettes in special cassette organizers, or stack them on narrow ledge shelves. Deep shelves provide too much space, and the cassettes can become a loose jumble. Vinyl records need to be stored correctly to prevent damage. Don't store them near heat sources such as radiators, lamps, or floor vents. Don't stack vinyl records; stand them on edge wherever you store them. You can put them on shelves, but the best place is a cabinet with a door that will keep the records away

from dust, dirt, and moisture. If your record collection is too much of a hassle, you can convert your records to CDs for a moderate expense. The CDs are much easier to store and more durable.

Entertaining Area

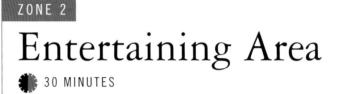

30 MINUTES

Below: A rattan chest serves as a coffee table in this entertainment lounge, holding seasonal linens and throw pillow covers. The reading chair and side chairs are positioned to view the TV, concealed in a pine wardrobe. The side tables are clustered with collections of photos so that nothing else can be put on them.

Opposite: A simple wood trunk can make a great coffee table. The interior offers a lot of long-term storage, and the shape provides stability to ensure that items like flower vases don't fall over when the table is bumped.

Your entertaining area can bring movies or music to life, but you need a comfortable place to watch or listen. This space is defined by the couch, coffee table, and surrounding chairs. The area may be focused on the entertainment center, but during parties or informal get-togethers, it can become a relaxed conversation pit where people cluster and socialize. The couch itself is rarely a clutter problem. Just keep throw pillows to a minimum—use only those that make you more comfortable. Groups of decorative pillows can too easily become a hiding place for remotes and other small items.

The heart of the entertaining area is the coffee table. It's the natural location for beverages and food, and serves as a parking place for books and magazines. A coffee table is indispensable for keeping things off the floor, and useful for short-term or specialized storage. Given its role as a centerpiece, choosing the right coffee table is essential to keeping the room organized.

➤ **COFFEE TABLE:** The first consideration in choosing a coffee table is style. You're probably not going to buy a coffee table that clashes with your other furnishings. But with a little investigation, you can find a piece that seamlessly integrates into your decor and still gives you the storage and organization space you need. The ideal coffee table provides enough surface space for beverages and food for the number of people who can fit in the entertaining area. It should also supply enough addi-

STORAGE IN STYLE

CONTROL REMOTES: No doubt you've experienced the frustration of the great remote-control hunt—especially now that you may have a remote for the TV, a remote for the VCR, and a remote for the DVD player. The reason remote controls go missing so often is that there isn't a place to put them. You can use your own containers, such as decorative pottery bowls or a nice tray, or choose from the many storage options in stores. Manufacturers provide a plethora of custom solutions for remotes. These include fancy remote carousels, simple plastic boxes with multiple cavities, elegant boxes with separate compartments for different remotes, and attractive wood caddies with space for remotes and TV listing guides.

A clear acrylic caddy keeps all your remote controls at your fingertips.

tional storage for everyday items such as magazines. In most cases, a shelf below the top is all the extra storage you'll need. But the coffee table can also provide drawers for items such as videotapes or the linens you use with a foldout sofa bed. If your needs are modest and you just want a place to put the remote and snacks, choose from traditional coffee tables. If your storage needs are more complicated, shop for nontraditional types.

Traditional coffee tables have fixed legs, a simple top, and a shelf or drawers underneath. Crafted of glass, wood, stone, or composite materials, these are meant only to provide a temporary resting place for food and drinks and basic items such as a television remote, a bowl of fruit, or magazines. The shelf or drawers add longer-term storage. A shelf is more accessible and more appropriate for visually attractive magazines or books. Drawers are better for organizing small items such as loose drink coasters or replacement batteries for remote controls. If you opt for drawers, remember to keep the drawers themselves organized with dividers or compartments; otherwise, their purpose is defeated.

Non-traditional coffee tables are increasingly in vogue. These can include cube-shaped boxes with lids, chests, or trunks, multitier units on casters, and other unusual versions. These are best matched to unusual storage needs. For instance, if you want to store seasonal throws near the couch for chilly nights, use a trunk coffee table with enough room for folded throws and maybe an extra pillow or two. Most types of unconventional coffee tables can function as mini closets to store board games, photo albums, or other items for which there is not enough shelf or closet space. One of the handiest types is an ottoman with a lid and hollow interior. When not being used with a chair, the ottoman can serve as a space-saving coffee table with significant storage under the lid.

ZONE 3

Reading Area

🕐 15 MINUTES

Family rooms and living rooms are made richer with a specific space where someone can spend an afternoon reading in leisurely comfort. The couch can certainly serve this purpose, but in most living rooms that have the space, a reading chair with a good reading light and small side table create a more intimate and suitable space. Set another chair across from the reading chair and the area can also function as an inviting conversational nook for parties or a place for couples to discuss the day's events. The clutter-busting requirement for this area is that the table be minimal—just enough room for a beverage and a book.

A reading area can be a cozy place for solitude and for enjoying a good book. It can also be kept clutter free by limiting the amount of space available to set down items.

Shelves

1 HOUR

Although shelves in a living room or family room are commonly devoted to books, they represent wonderful, flexible storage options for things that don't fit in the entertainment center or other locations in the room. From displays of pictures to boxes and albums of photos to candles and candleholders, shelves can keep a variety of items in order and in view. To make the most of the storage, shelf placement needs to be well thought out. Obviously, shelves can only be placed where they will fit, but they should also be placed as close as possible to where they will be used. For instance, a bookshelf will ideally be placed close to a reading chair and reading lamp. Available space and storage needs are the key determinants in what type of family- or living-room shelving you use.

Wall-mounted shelves fit in odd spaces, such as over sofas or above wainscoting. They are especially handy for keeping breakables,

Opposite: Wall shelves don't have to be boring to effectively organize books and other items. These contemporary "ladder" shelves are stylish and provide storage for small objects on top, and larger items on the bottom.

THE SHELF RULES

1. **Have a purpose.** Individual items must have a reason for being on the shelf. A picture is there to be displayed, and a candle is there to be lit on special occasions. Your eyeglasses shouldn't be there, nor should a pile of mail or the writing pad that includes the letter you've been working on.

2. **Collect to declutter.** Individual items that are part of a collection, such as figurines or a trio of decorative vases, should be grouped together in their own section of shelf. Alone they can become a part of shelf clutter.

3. **Contain when possible.** Some items you might like to put on a shelf are best kept within a box or other container. Perhaps you use a group of votives for parties and other special occasions. Rather than stack them loose, put them in a decorative wire basket or a handsome box at the end of a row of books.

such as a collection of glass vases or figurines, out of the reach of young children or out of the general traffic flow. You have more latitude in choosing the style of wall-mounted shelves because they are such small decorative elements. Don't use wall-mounted shelves for heavy objects, such as a row of coffee-table books; the chances of the shelf falling are just too great. Wall-mounted shelves with bookends or clamp-on edge stops are great alternatives to CD or DVD holders. They can be positioned to leave just the right amount of room for your music or movies, and they are often less expensive than buying a dedicated CD tower or rack.

Stand-alone shelves provide more substantial support and far more storage space than wall-mounted units. They also offer more design options. You can choose from enclosed shelving units that have a box frame and back piece, shelves with an outside frame but no backing, and shelves supported by a base and vertical braces. Where you need enclosed or hidden storage, pick shelving units that incorporate cabinets. In some cases, the floor or wall space where you want to locate the shelves is so awkward and oddly sized that finding a shelving unit is difficult. You can deal with this challenge by using tension-pole shelving systems. These use tension-pole supports that collapse or expand to fit varying distances between floor and ceiling. They are equipped with adjustable brackets. The shelves themselves are sold in different widths and depths, so you determine how wide a given column of shelves will be and how many columns you'll use. The shelf positions in these systems are completely movable, a handy feature for when you move things around and change what is kept on the shelves. If you're comfortable with a more permanent solution and have the money, you can have custom bookshelves built to your specifications.

Regardless of what type of shelf unit you use, organize books with the largest on the bottom shelves, and smallest on top. This keeps the shelf from tipping and is pleasing to the eye. To optimize shelf space, stack same-sized books vertically. They take up less shelf space than the same books aligned horizontally. You should also review your collection of books every 6 months or so to make sure you aren't dedicating space on your shelves to books you won't read and don't need. For instance, summer beach novels you've read can be removed and donated to a charity or a library.

ZONE 5

Fireplace and Mantel

15 MINUTES

A fireplace is a great luxury in the home, but the fireplace area—comprised of the fireplace and mantel—can be a casual resting place for a lot of what makes its way into living and family rooms. Where fireplaces are concerned, clutter invites clutter, so this is an area to keep as spartan as possible.

➤ FIREPLACE: The fireplace itself is rarely an organization problem. If you have a gas fireplace, you don't even need to worry about cleaning ashes or storing firewood. If you have a wood-burning fireplace, the brick or stone footing around the base of the fireplace should only be used for the fireplace accessories and perhaps a decorative urn or sculpture. Fireplace tools should be kept organized with a stand or separate hangers. Keep wood tidy in a large, fireproof wood basket, tin bucket, or metal cradle. Keep on hand only the wood you need for a single fire; too much wood means extra mess.

➤ MANTEL: Although it's a tempting ledge for all kinds of small items, keep the mantel as clear as possible. Use it as a showcase for one or two of your favorite decorative (fireproof) pieces. Put a cherished ceramic bowl in the center of the mantel, or place candles in heirloom candleholders at either end. The mantel is also a place for items relating to the function of the fireplace, such as a decorative match holder or fire igniter. Keep the mantel spare and people are less likely to absently place their eyeglasses or the cordless phone there. The less there is on the mantel, the more items that don't belong will stick out.

ZONE 6

Chests, Side Tables, and Supplementary Furniture

1 HOUR

By this point, you've got most of your living and family room in order. Now you need to determine what additional storage you need, and what other types of specialized furniture you want to complement the socializing, entertaining, or relaxing you do. Additional storage will probably be in the form of concealed space, in furniture such as chests or tables. These not only help with the storage in the living and family rooms, but can also provide long-term storage space for other rooms.

➤ CHESTS: A chest provides long-term storage and a place to sit, or a surface for decorative items or lighting. This can substitute for a linen closet, or serve as a handy location for seldom-used board games. A family-room chest is also a good place to display memorabilia, from pictures to awards to mementos of special occasions. The downside to using chests and trunks is their bulk and difficult access. They take up a lot of floor space, can block traffic flow, and are awkward to open and close. Use the top surface for storage or a collection of unbreakable decorations, to ensure that it doesn't become another clutter-collecting space.

DOLLAR SMART

BOOKED UP: Small tables can be useful and attractive additions to the living- or family-room layout, but there's no need to spend top dollar on a high-fashion table. Stack oversized coffee-table books that you've already read to make a nifty table for a reading light or remote-control holder. Use enough books for the height you want and you'll have a stable literary table to complement any decor!

➤ **TABLES:** Side tables and end tables are useful additions to the family and living rooms for both the surface and drawer or shelf space they provide. They can be strategically located to hold lamps where you need light the most—near chairs and other seating. They are useful for holding small items, such as phone books, near where these things are used.

➤ **BARS:** Keeping alcohol and drink accessories such as highball glasses, swizzle sticks, and cocktail shakers in the kitchen can make entertaining more a chore than a pleasure. But keeping bottles and accessories loose, on top of a table or other flat surface, invites spills and breakage, and creates a cluttered look. If your entertaining includes drinks, it's a good idea to keep a small bar trolley or caddy in the living or family room. Depending on how much wine, alcohol, and stemware you keep on hand, you can choose from many options, ranging from a simple two-shelf cart to a more elaborate stand-alone bar with pullout doors and compartments. Look for a unit that can fit neatly in a corner when not in use. If you have small children in the house, play it safe and buy bar furniture that lets you lock up the alcohol.

ZONE 7

Windowsills, Pianos, and Other Flat Surfaces

30 MINUTES

The many small, flat surfaces in a home seem to attract clutter like no place else. These surfaces are inviting "temporary" resting places for all the little things we carry from room to room in the house, from keys to eyeglasses to unopened mail. There are two basic strategies for keeping these surfaces clear of clutter. The first is the "no-vacancy" rule. This means keeping the surfaces bare at all times—anything that doesn't belong should be immediately removed. Unfortunately, in busy households, this may be a tough rule to maintain. A more appropriate strategy for busy homes is to create a focal point. Use the flat surface as a showcase area, with one central display. For instance, use your most beautiful vase full of dried flowers as the center of attention atop an upright piano. Put your favorite decorative ceramic bowl in the center of a windowsill (as long as it doesn't interfere with the opening of the window). Cluster a trio of unusual glass paperweights on a radiator cover. By creating a focal point, anything else put on the surface sticks out like a sore thumb.

KEEPING UP

The varied zones in living and family rooms call for a simple, clutter-busting maintenance strategy that can work across the space.

• **Two for one:** Integrate your "clutter check" as part of the regular dusting and vacuuming in the room. Return anything out of place to its proper location, especially if the location is in another room.

• **Periodical update:** Once a month, check the magazines and catalogs on your coffee table, and discard those that are out of date.

• **Disk order:** Every few months, make sure that your CDs and DVDs aren't piling up. If you need more storage space, buy an extra media tower or rack.

CHAPTER 5 | Dining Rooms

CONQUER CLUTTER ONE ZONE AT A TIME

1. Dining Table
2. Hutch or China Cabinet
3. Sideboard
4. Additional Storage

The dining room is one of the simpler rooms to organize. That's because the room is focused on one purpose: memorable meals. You might use the dining room for casual dining from time to time, but for the most part, the room is used for meals on special occasions. This includes holidays, celebrations such as birthdays, and times that you just want to have an intimate family meal.

This well-defined purpose leaves you with a clear goal in organizing the room: to make serving and enjoying meals as pleasant and simple as possible.

Your dining room may not necessarily be a separate room. In some homes, it's open floor space next to the kitchen, or at the end of a long living room. Whether a room in its own right or a space you carve out, the dining room is defined by the furniture you use there and the "service circle."

The service circle incorporates the dining table and the area around it. The circle includes where plates are stored, and where food is brought in and placed. In addition to the table, the service circle usually includes some sort of storage cabinet—from a simple hutch to a more ornate china cabinet—for fine dining pieces including crystal, china, and silver. If you have the floor space, the dining room should also include a sideboard or side table that provides additional storage underneath and a place on top to put food that won't fit or will get in the way on the table.

Opposite: A well-equipped dining room makes good use of a large hutch with ample serving surface, drawer space, and cabinet storage area.

Organize this room starting with the table. In each zone, remove everything that is currently stored there, and determine which items have something to do with serving, presenting, eating, or enjoying a meal. Those items that don't should be moved to another more appropriate part of the house, or should be given away. Once you've decided what needs to be stored in each zone, you'll know how much and what type of storage is required to completely organize the dining room.

E legance is the hall-mark of this simple, functional, and well-organized dining room.

A stylish corner hutch provides ample shelf space for signature pieces that deserve prominence. This open storage complements the concealed area in the sideboard. Note how a vase has been placed on top to ensure that the top surface doesn't become the resting place for incidental clutter.

The focal point in this dining room is a sturdy sideboard that offers a wide top surface for serving platters when needed, and a great deal of large and small storage options in the form of cabinets and drawers.

The table has been laid for tea, with a graceful runner and tea set. The setting is pleasing to the eye and can be left on the table permanently, discouraging anyone from setting other items on the table.

ZONE 1

Dining Table

🕐 15 MINUTES

The dining room table is for eating, drinking, and socializing after meals. Homework and school projects should be confined to work areas in kids' rooms. Bill paying and work-at-home tasks should be done in the home-office area. Activities other than dining can scratch the table and often leave behind clutter. As noted in the box to the right, reinforce the singular purpose of this room by keeping the table set to one degree or another. The idea is to dissuade anyone

This round table in a cozy dining room includes place settings that discourage clutter and add an element of elegance to the room.

THE INSIDE SCOOP

SPACE SHUFFLE: Not every homeowner is fortunate enough to have a kitchen that will accommodate a table for everyday meals. In some situations, the dining-room table must become the site of every meal. In these situations, the rules still apply—leave the table set (with durable place mats and everyday flatware) so that people are deterred from leaving clutter on the table between meals. Keep the centerpiece on the table to add a bit of elegance to each meal.

HIDE A LEAF: If you're considering a new dining-room table and need one that can adapt to larger and smaller groups, shop for one with self-storing leaves. The most common are those with "butterfly" leaves that simply fold in and slide under the surface of the table. Self-storing leaves eliminate the need to find a safe place to put them, and are easier to use.

from using the table for something other than dining.

The central storage issue concerning the dining-room table is what to do with the leaves and pads, if any (obviously not an issue if you have a glass dining-room table). A closet near the dining room—especially a closet that doesn't see much use—is the ideal location for removable table leaves. Wherever you put them, it should be someplace where they are unlikely to get scratched or to experience extremes of hot or cold, or to be exposed to water. If your dining room is spacious, consider keeping your extra table leaves in the table.

ZONE 2

Hutch or China Cabinet

1 HOUR

A place for china, crystal, silver, and other precious dinnerware is an essential part of any formal dining room. The traditional hutch or china cabinet is both showcase and storage. It's a place to put signature or heirloom pieces on display, and one to hide dining-room essentials such as linens, serving trays, and sterling silverware. Hutches and cabinets come in lots of different sizes and shapes, but the purpose is the same: to organize all the things you'll use for eating and drinking. These include plates, glasses, cups, special dishes, and utensils. Because most of what you store in a hutch has both sentimental and real-dollar value, leave plenty of room around individual items to

STORAGE IN STYLE

CORNER STORE: If space is tight in your dining room, consider using a corner hutch or hutches. These triangular cabinets nestle into the corner of the room and are an efficient use of space and a way to keep valuables out of the flow of traffic in the room. Two of these placed in adjacent corners can provide about the same amount of storage as a standard-sized hutch. They are also great for displaying your favorite fine china, family heirloom pieces, and treasured teacups.

protect against breakage. As with other rooms and zones in the house, a key principle in organizing the hutch or china cabinet is to organize items by type.

➤ CHINA: Fine china is durable enough to withstand decades of use, but delicate enough that improper storage can cause chipping or scratching. The three basic ways to store china are stacking, racking, and packing. How you store yours depends on the type of space you have and if you want to display the china. Even though you may choose different storage methods for different pieces, try to keep all your china grouped close together—but not too close, to avoid chipping—including ancillary pieces such as gravy boats and butter trays.

Stack china where it is unlikely to receive any kind of blow to the edges of plates and saucers or lips of cups. Place buffer sheets between stacked plates to protect them from scratching one another. Buffers can be felt pads, cardboard squares, or even thick cloth napkins. Never stack china cups. Line them up in rows.

Racks for plates and dishes make efficient use of storage space. These are simple wood or plastic frames with slots that hold plates apart from one another and prevent scratching and chipping. They are made to sit securely on cabinet shelves and organize plates so that you can easily remove them as needed. Use softwood shelf racks that can accommodate your entire set of plates and saucers. The best racks protect china by providing an individual slot for each plate or saucer. Choose a rack with a shelf for rows of china cups, so all your china can be kept together. Don't confuse these storage racks with wall-mounted display racks. Wall-mounted racks should be used to display specialty pieces or small groups of attractive serving plates—not whole sets of china.

Pack away china when there is not enough room for it in display storage, or if you use it infrequently and want to ensure against any breakage. Inexpensive, quilted china-packing cases come in all shapes and sizes to accommodate the number and size of pieces in

Below left: A country-style hutch provides all the storage a dining room needs, including glass-front cabinets for cups and dinnerware, large drawers for linens, and a thick bottom shelf for oversize serving pieces.

Below right: A built-in corner hutch provides a lot of storage for plate racks with a cabinet below, without taking any floor space away in this formal and elegant dining room.

your collection. These have zippered openings to keep dust and dirt away from your china while it is in storage. Keep the packed china in the cabinet area of your hutch.

➤ CRYSTAL: The surface of fine crystal is softer and more prone to scratching than regular glass. This means you need to leave plenty of room around your crystal pieces, regardless of whether they are small creamers and cordial glasses or larger pieces such as vases. Never store something inside a piece of crystal. Crystal stemware is most fragile along the stem, so don't hang it from stemware racks. Since the rim of crystal glassware is fragile, store glasses standing upright, with plenty of room around them to prevent breakage. Avoid keeping crystal on or under adjustable shelves; any jostling of the shelf can cause expensive breakage. You can also store crystal in padded boxes or containers, such as the ones used for china. But open storage lets you show off some of your most beautiful glassware.

STORAGE IN STYLE

HERB HELP: Protect your linens and keep them smelling lovely with a little help from the garden. Dried lavender sprigs in the folds of your dining-room linens will repel insects and perfume the fabric.

Plate racks are a handy way to store your favorite dishes, and this simple hutch includes them with hanging pegs, cabinet space, and a serving area.

➤ **SILVER:** Sterling silver is extremely sensitive to its environment. To protect your silverware and serving pieces from tarnish and corrosion, store them correctly. First and foremost, keep silver pieces out of circulating air. Store your silver away from other metals, in a silverware chest or box. These are made with tarnish-resistant liners and cavities for the different pieces in your set. You can also put the silver in tarnish-resistant storage bags, but keep the bags out of the sun and away from dampness. It's usually best to keep the silverware in its container in a hutch cabinet or drawer. But many silverware boxes are relatively airtight and are crafted of attractive hardwoods, so you may want to keep the box on a shelf or on top of the sideboard.

➤ **LINENS:** You can certainly store your special-occasion tablecloths and fine napkins in a linen closet or wherever you put your bed linens. But in keeping with the idea of storing items near where they're used, it's best to stow dining-room linens in the dining room. Place these in the concealed area of the hutch (or the sideboard, if you don't have room in the hutch), and put cedar blocks with the linens to deter insects. Don't place fine linens directly on a wood shelf, because the wood and its finish may contain acids that will discolor the cloth over time. Use a shelf liner or keep your linens in a box. Heirloom lace and embroidered tablecloths should be wrapped in acid-free paper for maximum protection. Find the paper in art supply or fabric stores. You should regularly rotate and refold your linens to prevent creases from becoming permanent.

ZONE 3

Sideboard

⚙ 30 MINUTES

The role of the sideboard is to hold food while serving, and to store vessels and utensils used in serving food. The ideal dining-room sideboard includes an uncluttered top surface and ample storage below in the form of shelves or cabinets. The top surface is a utility area, and the lower part of the sideboard holds the workhorses of memorable meals.

➤ **TABLETOP:** The top surface of a sideboard provides a place to put large serving dishes from the kitchen that wouldn't otherwise fit on the dining-room table during meals. It can be very useful in this role, as a place for dish warmers to keep food warm or a place to put the remains of a course as you move to the next one. It's also a place to work with food, such as cutting a large sheet cake, that would be difficult on the dining table itself. In between meals, the top serves as a location for those special items you don't want to keep on the table, such as a candelabra and salt-and-pepper or cream-and-sugar sets. The common thread that all these items share is utility. If it isn't used for a meal, it doesn't belong on the sideboard.

➤ **LOWER STORAGE:** The shelves or cabinets underneath the sideboard's top should be dedicated to oversized serving items. These include punch bowls; large, decorative serving trays; serving bowls; and special oversized pitchers. This can also be a great place to store linens, but don't place them touching other items or the wood shelf or they may become stained.

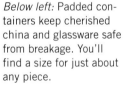

Below left: Padded containers keep cherished china and glassware safe from breakage. You'll find a size for just about any piece.

Below right: Prevent silver from tarnishing with special anti-tarnish felt bags.

Additional Storage

⏱ 30 MINUTES

Depending on the size and capacity of your hutch and sideboard, you may need to find extra storage space for small seasonal items, replacement supplies, and other items that just don't fit in those zones. Because there is rarely enough room around a table—given the space needed to comfortably pull chairs in and out—more furniture is usually not the answer. Instead, turn to wall space for additional dining-room storage.

Below: A special bar drawer built into a hutch provides a discreet place for alcohol, mixers, and accessories such as wine openers and cocktail napkins.

Opposite: An elegant cabinet provides excellent storage in the dining room, as well as a place to keep and display stemware.

Shelves can provide attractive, much-needed storage positioned out of traffic flow. Use shelves to store decorative boxes containing supplies such as festive special-occasion napkin rings and backup candles, or as display storage for collections such as spoons or demitasse cups. Or use them to hold seasonal centerpieces or candle holders that don't fit on top of the sideboard. Special ledge shelves with a thin, routed channel are excellent for storing and displaying sets of three or four plates, or larger ceramic serving dishes.

Hanging plate racks are a way to store your special serving dishes or dessert plates while creating decorative interest on the wall. You can select from wrought-iron types that provide a frame for the plates, more discreet wire hangers that let the plate "float" on the wall, or simple wood types. Just make sure you hang the plates where they won't get bumped.

Wine racks are a natural addition to the dining room, placing the beverage where it will most likely be consumed. Because the vast majority of wines—especially moderately priced versions—are drinkable immediately and don't benefit from aging, you should only keep on hand the wine you'll use for one or two parties or dinners. Position your wine rack out of direct sunlight and away from any heat sources such as heating vents or high-intensity track lights.

A single folding table provides a place for wine bottles, hanging storage for goblets, and a serving tray.

Always store bottles on their sides, so the cork stays moist, preventing oxygen from reaching the wine. The average temperature range in a home is not optimal for wine, but won't cause any noticeable deterioration over a period of a few months. If you're looking to store wine longer, consider the basement (see page 141) or use a wine refrigerator.

KEEPING UP

The dining room is generally out of the traffic flow of the house, making it one of the easier rooms to keep free of clutter. Maintenance is still important, however.

Dining-room beat: Every few days, walk through the dining room and do a clutter inspection to ensure that nobody has left items on the dining-room table or sideboard. Remove whatever you find, placing it back where it belongs.

CHAPTER 6

Basements and Attics

Even though the basement and attic are two distinct rooms, they are grouped here because they share a central purpose—to provide long- and short-term storage for other areas of the house. The other reason to group the two is that many houses don't have both. That's why you should approach the zones in this chapter according to your home's layout and your individual needs. Some zones, such as the emergency area, should be present in every house. Others, such as workshop space, may or may not be included, depending on your lifestyle. Choose the zones that apply to you and organize them in an order that makes sense for your circumstances.

As alike as the rooms may be, the location of the zones takes into account the fundamental differences between basements and attics. Basements are generally easier to access, so supplies such as beverages and food bought in bulk are more logically stored there. But basements are also damp, so anything prone to mold and mildew, such as clothing, finds a more fitting home in the attic.

Whether you have an attic, basement, or both, the first step toward organizing the space is removing everything that is currently there, and doing a thorough cleaning. As unpleasant as this may sound, it's essential because these rooms are prone to insect and rodent infestation. If you have pest problems, you need to deal with them before organizing the space, or you'll just wind up making a mess of your newly clutter-free room once you're forced to deal with the problem.

Clearing everything out also gives you the chance to winnow out boxes and belongings that you no longer need or want. Donate or discard these.

Opposite: While most attics are used for storage, this previously unused space was turned into an attractive extra bedroom for overnight guests. The wood slats on the closet doors blend in with the walls to give the room a clean look.

The general rule of assigning specific locations to what you store applies in the basement and attic more than any other room in the house. Because the central purpose of these rooms is storage, you need to make it as simple and quick as possible for anyone to find anything in the space. Keeping everything in its own section also helps ensure the things that see occasional use, such as holiday decorations, will be put back in good order.

In some instances, you'll have to transfer a given zone to a different room. For instance, hazardous materials must be stored under lock and key. But those that would normally be centralized in a basement can go into a locked garage cabinet if your home doesn't have a basement. The principles outlined still apply.

Although you should clean out the basement in one session, don't try to organize the whole space at once—there's simply too great a chance that you'll fall behind and will have to start over. When you're organizing the zones, don't get ambitious; take them one at a time. The times assigned to each zone are fairly standard, regardless of how big or small your basement or attic might be, but the times can be considerable, as you'll see.

These zone guidelines don't apply to converted attics or basements. If you have turned a dry basement into an extra bedroom or a child's playroom, or finished the attic for use as a home office, consult the appropriate chapter for organization strategies that relate to those rooms.

ZONE 1

Basement Emergency Area

🔆 1 HOUR

Homeowners in today's world must be prepared for natural and terrorist disasters. The first step is to create a home emergency kit and store it in the basement, where you and your family should gather in the event of an emergency. (If you don't have a basement, keep the kit in a room with few windows and other openings; you should be able to block the few you have with duct tape and plastic sheeting.) The U.S. Department of Homeland Security (www.dhs.org) recommends that homeowners keep a 3-day supply of food and water on hand for each member of the household. The government specifically recommends the following items.

➤ WATER: At least 3 gallons of water per person, sealed in plastic jugs.

➤ FOOD: An adequate supply of canned and dried food for each person, for at least 3 days.

➤ CLOTHES: One change of clothes for each person in the house.

➤ SUPPLIES: These should include a flashlight, a battery-powered radio, extra batteries, a complete first aid kit, toilet articles, backup prescription medicines, a can opener, and duct tape and heavy-duty garbage bags to seal windows and doors. You should also include a wrench (to turn off utilities), dust masks, and moist hand and face wipes.

Store the emergency supplies in a clearly designated, accessible area. Keep all the supplies for the kit in sealed, clear plastic tubs, and mark them with the label "Emergency Kit." Include a list of emergency contacts in the kit.

THE INSIDE SCOOP

ACTIVITY ZONE: Although not required by the Department of Homeland Security, adding one or two board games or even a pack of cards to your emergency kit can help you during a crisis. One of the many challenges when disaster strikes is dealing with hours of boredom while waiting for the situation to improve. Games provide you with a way to pass the time and keep your mind off the emergency itself. Books can help ease the boredom, too.

ZONE 2

Basement Workshop

⚙ 1 HOUR

The basement can be a wonderful, quiet refuge for spending time on a hobby or home-improvement project. Use the space as a simple crafts corner where you create handmade holiday decorations, or set up a more a complex work area to accommodate the sophisticated equipment necessary for a home darkroom or jewelry-making operation. The keys to getting the most out of your home workshop are a physical setup that lets you work smoothly without creating clutter, and safety elements that ensure your hobby presents no danger to you or your family.

➤ **WORKTABLE:** The two major requirements of a good worktable are that it provide adequate space—so your supplies and equipment aren't cramped—and that it be sturdy. You can choose from wood, metal, or plastic tables, but wood is often the best choice. Wood tables are usually forgiving of spills and other accidents, and it's fairly easy to make a crude wood table to fit your needs with just a little plywood and 4 two-by-fours. Because most hobbies involve a sequential process, you should set up the table to facilitate your workflow. For instance, a basement darkroom should be set up with the enlarger on the left, and the developer, rinse, and fix trays in that order to the right. There should be enough room between pieces of equipment to allow necessary free movement.

➤ **SHELVES AND CABINETS:** Most basement work areas benefit from the addition of shelves or cabinets. Mount shelves to hold frequently used supplies such as hot-glue sticks and poster paint for general crafts, or solder for jewelry making. Metal shelves are the best choice for work areas because they are durable, lightweight, nonabsorbent (making them easy to clean), and easy to install. Cabinets are perfect for storing chemicals and other supplies or

STORAGE IN STYLE

TOOL'S GOLD: A handyman's tool belt is a remarkably versatile tool holder that can hold many different types of hobby tools. Hang it across the front of your workbench to keep tools close at hand or suspend the belt overhead from the rafters, if that is more convenient.

equipment that could pose a health risk. If you have children in the house, keep the cabinet locked. Depending on the space you have, use a standing cabinet or one mounted on the wall to the side of the worktable. Whether you are using shelves, a cabinet, or both, supplies and equipment should be separated and organized by type, to make it easy to find what you need when you need it.

➤ TOOL STORAGE: Tools and their accessories, such as drill bits, must be conveniently organized to avoid clutter and to keep them from getting lost. Some tool sets come with a stand-alone rack that keeps the items in order. If the tools for your hobby don't have their own rack, you'll need to create or buy a holder for them. The goal with any tool organizer is to keep tools close at hand. That way you can grab them when you need them, and you'll quickly get in the

This basement workshop is kept in order with locking cabinets, tool drawers, and an integrated work surface. Outdoor tools are hung on the walls, freeing up space in the garage.

THE INSIDE SCOOP

FLAME KILLERS: Whether protecting against flammable hobby materials or common household accidents such as grease fires, it's wise to keep the right fire extinguisher in close proximity to areas that present fire dangers. Extinguishers are rated for the types of fires they fight: "Class A" for common combustibles such as wood and paper; "Class B" for fire caused by flammable liquids such as gasoline or grease; and "Class C" for electrical fires. ("Class D" are special extinguishers for use on flammable metals and are not usually used in the home.) New labeling shows graphic symbols of the type of fire the extinguisher should be used on. Multiclass extinguishers—rated "ABC"—are the preferred choice for the home because they extinguish the widest range of fires.

habit of putting them back right where they belong. Choose from "hobby" cases that are great for small items, such as supplies for tying fishing flies; basic toolboxes; wall-mounted, magnetic tool-holders, or stepped benchtop organizers.

As part of organizing your work area, you'll need to include safety features where necessary to make your projects risk free.

➤ **VENTILATION:** Many home hobbies involve unhealthy fumes that should be ventilated from the confined space of the basement. Vapors from photography darkroom chemicals, fumes from metal-finishing products, and soldering fumes from small plumbing projects can all be toxic. Proper ventilation requires both a source for fresh air and a fan to vent fumes. A fan stuck in a window isn't sufficient. Look for basic ventilation systems—usually consisting of an exhaust fan, ductwork (such as flexible tubing), and a hood—at large home centers or home-heating companies. Select one with the proper cfm (cubic feet per minute) rating and hood design for the size of your space.

➤ **FIRE SAFETY:** Many pastimes require working with an open flame or flammable materials. These include stained-glass crafting, wood etching, and others. If your hobby involves fire dangers, mount the appropriate fire extinguisher in clear view as close as possible to the work area. Keep the route to the fire extinguisher, and to basement exits, clear at all times. Familiarize yourself with the instructions because a fire is the worst time to learn how to use an extinguisher.

➤ **WASTE DISPOSAL:** Most chemicals used in hobbies should not be dumped directly down your drain. Substances that require special disposal include containers that hold the residue from wood stain or oil-based paints and thinners, darkroom "fix" solution, metal solvents, and machine oils. You also need to follow local guidelines in disposing of any solids containing lead or other toxic heavy metals.

Keep these substances in appropriate containers. Take them to your local hazardous waste disposal center (contact your sanitation department for storage and disposal guidelines and the location of your hazardous waste facility).

ZONE 3

Basement Hazardous Material Storage

30 MINUTES

Hazardous materials include cleaning supplies that could be dangerous to small children and pets, flammable materials such as paint thinner, and pesticides. These should be kept in a locked cabinet, clearly marked with the contents. A metal cabinet is better than a wood unit because metal won't soak up spills and isn't flammable. Position the cabinet out of the general traffic flow in the basement. Clearly mark the cabinet so that any emergency personnel responding to a fire will quickly see what's in the cabinet.

Building supplies, materials, and equipment are kept organized in this three section shelf-and-cabinet unit. Hazardous materials are kept locked in the cabinet.

Basement Food and Beverage Storage

1 HOUR

Positioned far from work and hazardous material storage areas, the food zone in your basement is a backup to your pantry, one that lets you take advantage of the significant discounts available in price clubs. The requirements for this type of storage are that the food and beverage be up off the floor, in an area that is easy to get to, and that the storage support be stable and large enough to handle all your bulk buys. Shelves are the preferred option for storing food, because you can see the inventory you have on hand. Position stored goods in order of weight—canned goods and beverages on the lower shelves, other dry goods and plastics on the upper shelves.

➤ **DRY AND CANNED FOODS:** Just as you did in the pantry, group foods by type in basement storage. You should also be strict about rotating stock. Placing newer purchases in back of old ensures that you use the freshest ingredients and helps you detect and remedy any rodent problems before the damage is excessive. Because of the basement's high humidity, dry-goods packaging should be nonabsorbent. If you want to store materials that are in absorbent packaging, you'll need to transfer them to plastic bins or tubs with tight-fitting lids to protect against mold. Allow for plenty of air circulation around the stored goods.

➤ **GENERAL BEVERAGES:** Whenever possible, keep canned and bottled beverages in their cases. Try to store larger economy-size bottles or jugs in a row by type of beverage. The aim is to prevent tipping and spills. Don't leave open beverage containers in the basement—they are an invitation to pests and a spill waiting to happen. If you've bought tall, thin bottles, keep them grouped in a shallow plastic tray or bin. This will not only help prevent spills, it will also contain any that do occur. Clean any spills promptly so as to avoid attracting insects. Beverage storage should always be located away from any basement heat sources such as dryer vents, boilers, hot-water pipes, and so on.

➤ **WINE:** The basement is often the perfect place to store a wine collection. Wine is best kept in relative dark, at a consistent temperature around 55°F, with humidity around 70 to 80 percent. Keep your wine away from basement windows and far from heat sources such as a boiler or hot-water pipes. Store the wine by type to make it easy to find the bottle you want. Don't keep wine bottles in their original cardboard cases. The cardboard is too likely to absorb moisture and weaken over time.

Box racks are a traditional type of wine storage constructed with a wood outside frame and crisscrossing interior wood shelves that form diamond- or square-shaped cubbies for the bottles. These look nice, are extremely stable, and the units can be stacked, a handy feature when you want to expand your wine collection. The only drawback is that it is difficult to see the wine labels without pulling out the bottles. It's wise to keep the racks up off the floor just in case the basement ever floods. Put them on cinder blocks or stack them on a sturdy table.

Shelf racks are more adaptable. These expandable shelving units are freestanding, with slots for the bottles. The racks can be stacked row by row to slowly increase storage as needed. Although not as stable as box racks, most shelf-rack designs let you view the label without pulling out the bottle. Shelf racks are available in wood, metal, and plastic. Metal racks of any type must be coated with a rust-inhibiting finish if they will be used in the basement.

STORAGE IN STYLE
PIPE DREAM: Although it's okay to hang storage from the joists in the basement, hanging anything from a plumbing pipe puts stress on the connections and can easily lead to a leak. Even if the pipe seems to be held firmly in place with brackets, don't hang anything from it.

Basement General Shelving and Cabinets

30 MINUTES

The basement offers a place to put overflow from the garage or garden shed, and can accommodate odds and ends from the household as well. Shelves are excellent for storing seasonal items, such as plastic plant-pots and hoses, that would not fare well in the winter temperatures of a garage or shed. If space is limited in your garage—or if you don't have a garage—the basement can provide space to store supplies such as lawn fertilizer and plant food, and equipment such as sprinklers. Be aware that bagged materials such as potting soil and manure are prone to leaks. If you keep these materials in the basement, consider transferring them to 5 gallon plastic buckets (the type restaurants use). You can purchase these buckets, with lids, at home centers and nurseries. Hang hoses brought in for the winter from hooks affixed to joists.

A basement benefits from this easy-to-clean cabinet, used here for laundry supplies. Fitting snugly in a corner, the unit can be locked to keep toxic materials away from children and pets.

Attic Clothing Storage

🕐 1 HOUR

As diligent as you might be about weeding out your wardrobe on a regular basis, you will inevitably need to store some clothing. You may want to put away your first child's little-used clothes, so that a younger sibling can wear them in the future. Or you may want to keep favorite outfits from when your child was very young. Certain clothes of yours are keepsakes, too. For instance, you might save your wedding dress so that your daughter can wear it. Depending on what part of the country you live in, you'll need to rotate seasonal clothing in and out of storage. Whatever the situation, an attic can prove invaluable for keeping clothes in good shape over a long period of time. Whether storing clothing on hangers or in a box, make sure the articles are completely clean before putting them away; even a little dirt can create bad odors and attract insects over time.

THE CLOTHES STORAGE RULES

1. **Remove accessories.** Jewelry and decorative ornamentation on clothing can cause rips and tears and, depending on the jewelry, can stain other garments.

2. **Empty pockets.** Loose change, keys, or other items stored in pockets of a garment can cause permanent distortion of the fabric.

3. **Button up.** Close all fasteners on clothing, including buttons, zippers, and snaps, to help the garment maintain its proper shape.

4. **Clean first.** Dry-clean or wash clothes one last time, rinsing well to ensure that stains are gone and that no lasting traces of scented detergent or bleach—which can damage stored garments—remain. Never starch clothes before storing; it can cause yellowing and attract insects.

5. **Bag free.** Do not store clothing in plastic bags. Plastic traps moisture and can cause mold and mildew.

> **FOLDED CLOTHES:** Be sure to fold clothes carefully for long-term storage so you don't damage the articles. Use the right size and number of boxes for the clothes you are storing; cramming clothes into an undersized box will only lead to permanent crease marks and fabric deterioration. The type of box can also have an effect on the clothes. Look for waterproof, vented plastic boxes for clothes other than wool garments. Store wool pieces in cedar chests, with lids that seal tightly. Protect clothes in plastic or cardboard boxes against insect damage by putting in mothballs, cedar blocks, or lavender sachets. Make sure the boxes are sealed well, or the insect repellants won't work. As an extra precaution, include a drying agent such as silica gel, which will absorb moisture and prevent mold and mildew from ruining clothes. Precious clothes and heirlooms, such as a lace tablecloth, should be wrapped in acid-free tissue paper—and the box should be lined with acid-free paper—that you can find in art stores and at many dry cleaners. To make your life a little easier, organize garments within their boxes so that sweaters are grouped

Below left: A handy portable closet is essential for attic clothing storage. This one features fabric panels that zip shut to protect against dust and dirt, and a shelf over the hanging rods.

Below right: A simple rolling hanging bar is a quick solution for short-term clothes storage in the attic. A bottom shelf lets you store flat items such as the plastic shoe-box shown here.

THE WHEEL THING: For easy access to seasonal clothes you want to store outside the bedroom, consider a rolling closet. The closet will stop when it hits a slanted attic ceiling, presenting the opportunity to position boxed clothes behind the hanging garments, in the angled space behind the closet. The best rolling closets have canvas or fabric covers with all-around zippers and cedar floors. If the attic is equipped with a closet, put hanging garments in their own canvas storage bags.

with sweaters, children's clothes are grouped by size and article, and so on. Make it easy to find the clothes you need, and ensure that the boxes don't migrate to another part of the attic, by affixing labels. Duct tape marked with permanent ink markers makes for long-lasting labels.

➤ **HANGING CLOTHES:** Some clothes, such as dresses and coats, should be hung to maintain their shape and fabric. Vented fabric garment bags with zippers and opaque, insect-resistant linings are ideal for precious clothes that you want to protect as thoroughly as possible.

Attic Memorabilia Space

🔴 1 HOUR

Some memorabilia have sentimental and historical value, such as your father's war medals or the samplers your great grandmother made. Others have monetary value, such as antique statues or stained-glass panels handed down through generations. Some memorabilia have both. Attic memorabilia include the personal souvenirs you've collected over time and family heirlooms that you don't want to display for any number of reasons. The goal is to protect it all against breakage and deterioration. Lined and padded memory chests are ideal containers for your precious memorabilia. These come in a variety of sizes, with compartments, drawers, pullout bins, and other configurations. Pick the one that best accommodates what you need to store. If you decide to put your memorabilia in plain plastic or cardboard boxes, make sure all breakables are thoroughly padded, and buy opaque boxes that will prevent light from fading the colors in fabrics and painted pieces.

Attic Holiday Decorations

⏱ 15 MINUTES

Attic storage is ideal for delicate—and not so delicate—holiday decorations. Once largely limited to Christmas ornaments and lights, decorations these days may include fake skeletons for Halloween, Thanksgiving centerpieces and candles, and even Fourth of July banners and yard decorations. Themed decorating has become a part of just about every major holiday. To make sure your decorations stay in good shape the rest of the year, dedicate a corner of the attic to them. If you use decorations for only one or two holidays, just stack them in a column of boxes. If you have a bigger collection of holiday decorations, use standing shelves to keep everything in one place. Don't store decorations loose. You can find a specialized box or container for just about any type of decoration. For instance, wreaths can be put away in protective storage bags or octagonal boxes custom made for wreaths.

A decorative ornament box brings a splash of fashion to the attic. The box comes equipped with dividers to hold ornaments separately, and a zip-up plastic cover.

A durable plastic ornament box can be the best option where the box is likely to see rough treatment and protecting against breakage is the goal.

➤ **ORNAMENTS:** You'll find an amazing diversity of options when it comes to storing Christmas ornaments. Specialized boxes abound, most with individual compartments for each ornament. You can select from padded cardboard boxes, fancy molded-plastic units, or even wood chests. Choose ornament boxes based on how much you're willing to spend and how precious your collection is— wood chests offer the most protection but cost the most. Plastic is durable and will absorb shocks when the box is moved around, but if there is little traffic in the attic, a cardboard ornament box may provide all the protection you need. The most important element in your choice is buying a container that will store the number of ornaments you have.

➤ **DECORATIVE LIGHTS:** Strings of festive lights have long been a part of the Christmas celebration, and tangled masses of light strings have been the aftermath of many a holiday season. Keep your strings of lights tidy with a spool light-string organizer. If you have several strings, such as outdoor sets and the sets you use on the tree, you can buy special plastic storage boxes with slots for each organizer and cavities for extra bulbs.

Attic General Storage

🕐 30 MINUTES

Color-coded boxes make organizing boxes in the attic a much easier chore.

Extra room in the attic can serve as long-term storage for records and files that need to be kept for legal or tax reasons. Files should be kept in file-holder boxes, with built-in supports that keep the files upright and organized. Label the boxes and stack them neatly in the most out-of-the-way corner in the attic. Legal documents and important papers that you want to store in the attic should be kept in a fire-proof or fire-resistant box or safe.

KEEPING UP

Basements and attics often become the dumping grounds for household goods that have no place else to go. Consequently, you need to be vigilant in these areas. Every six months or so, conduct an organizational review of your basement and attic to make sure the zones are still in order.

• **Emergency update:** Every 3 months, check your emergency supplies to confirm that batteries are still good, equipment is functioning, and food and water supplies are not leaking or damaged.

• **Seasonal survey:** With the change of seasons, check on clothing in long-term storage to ensure that it is still neatly organized, and that no moths or other insects or rodents have gotten to the clothes. Check to make sure that boxes are still stacked in a logical order.

CHAPTER 7

Garages and Sheds

Garages and sheds are traditionally rough, unfinished spaces, exposed to greater variations in temperature and humidity than the house itself. These structures are best suited for storing equipment and supplies that are normally used outside, such as power tools, gardening equipment, outdoor furniture, and sports gear. Although attached garages are a slightly different case, and usually maintain a temperature and humidity range closer to the inside of the house, they follow the same principles. All the information for zones in this chapter pertains equally to sheds and garages.

Organizing a garage or outbuilding is a matter of "sectionalizing." Each type of equipment or supplies will get a specific section of wall or floor space, clearly separate from other sections. This way, you will be able to easily determine where things go. However, some outdoor structures are so small that they are limited to one type of storage, such as garden tools and supplies. In that case, use the guidelines for that particular zone.

Just starting the process is usually the hardest part of organizing a garage or shed. Garages tend to become household dumping grounds. That's why before you start organizing the zones of the garage you need to pull everything out. Choose a day when the weather is good, and plan to spend a couple of hours just emptying the garage and sweeping it out. Get rid of all the things you don't need, and determine what stays in the garage and what should go elsewhere. Once you've created a clean, blank slate to work with, start planning the zones you'll use.

Note that the times listed for these zones assume a full house of active people. You may do much less gardening and fewer outdoor

Opposite: Garages are versatile spaces that can be set up with many different storage options. Here, gardening tools on Peg Board share space with gardening equipment on a work table and shelves.

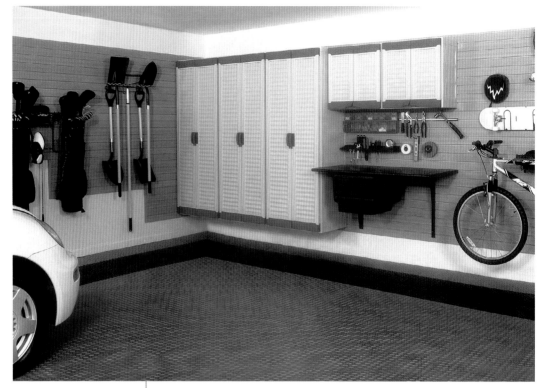

THE INSIDE SCOOP

COMPLETE SOLUTION: Garage wall systems are a way to organize the entire garage at once. These systems use standardized slotted wall panels that are hung in rows on the garage wall studs (metal studs are installed in the case of masonry walls). You then choose from a range of specially designed benches, cabinets, shelves, and accessories that are constructed to hang from the slots in the wall panels. This gives you the opportunity to customize garage storage to suit your needs. Although fairly expensive, the systems can be a quick all-in-one solution for the homeowner. Most companies offer the panels and hanging structures with or without installation and wall-system planning services.

STORAGE IN STYLE

FALSE ATTIC: Create a simple, concealed overhead storage space in the garage by laying thin plywood sheets across the overhead joists that span the width of the garage. This gives you additional long-term storage for any overflow from your attic.

activities; in this case, you can expect to scale back the amount of time each zone will take.

Obviously, your garage may not include all the zones listed. For instance, you may have no interest in sports, or maybe tools aren't a storage challenge, because you prefer to call a repairman. But whatever zones you include, lay out a plan for accommodating them in your garage. Using a pad and pencil, or chalk to mark the garage floor, decide which zones go where. Sketch out the sections, or mark their boundaries. Then start organizing zone by zone.

Opposite: A wall system can be an all-in-one garage storage solution. The companies that make these systems sell easily-installed wall panels with slots for hanging accessories—you simply choose the ones that fit your needs. As shown here, the wall-mounted fixtures range from simple racks to complete cabinet units, worktables, and more.

A space-saving recycling tower keeps recyclables in order, with three handy bins that pop out for curbside service and cleaning.

ZONE 1

Recycling Center

30 MINUTES

It's often surprising how messy a few weeks' accumulation of newspapers and recycled containers can be. Uncontained, newspapers can drift around the garage; glass and cans for recycling can quickly overflow undersized containers. The trick is to designate a recycling area that includes containers with much greater capacity than you will normally need. Then, when you fail to recycle in a timely manner, you won't be stuck with a huge mound of clutter. The first step is to identify the recycling area in your garage. For most homes, the best area is right next to the door leading into the garage. The area needs to be large enough for newspaper, glass, and metal recycling containers. Next, you need to choose appropriate containers. Most municipalities require that you separate recyclables into paper products, glass and plastics, and metals. Think about how much of these materials you collect between recycling pickup days. Check what your town requires, then pick up appropriate containers that provide enough room for you to miss one recycling pickup. To make things easier, choose different colors of containers and label them in large letters (unless your municipality already requires that certain colors be used for different recyclables). If you're willing to spend the money, you can buy premade recycling centers, with bins that are contained in their own framework. The top-of-the-line structures have lids and include bins that tilt out. But you can certainly make do with separate bins as long as they are the right size. For a household with few people, you may need only shallow plastic tubs. For a family of four or more people, you may need small garbage cans.

ZONE 2

ZONE 2

Hand Tools

🕐 30 MINUTES

Almost every homeowner has experienced the frustration of looking high and low for a particular hand tool needed to complete a home repair. Small but crucial, hand tools too easily slip into cracks and crevices, drop behind the worktable, or disappear mysteriously when they don't have their own clearly identified home. That's why organizing your hand tools is a huge step in making your life easier (and in saving money on replacing those that seem to drift away).

THE HAND TOOL QUESTIONS

1. Do you centralize your home repair tools at a bench in the garage? If so, Peg Board tool storage may be the most efficient way to store your tools and keep them ready for use.

2. Do you own a great number and/or diversity of tools, such as car repair and general home repair tools? A large, rolling chest can provide a lot of separate compartments for tools of different sizes and shapes. Combine this with a smaller toolbox for frequently used tools like common sizes of screwdrivers, hammers, and pliers.

3. Are your tools extremely valuable? If you have pricey tools, such as vintage woodworking chisels and planes, store them in locked cabinets or boxes.

➤ **HANGING STORAGE:** Decades ago, home handymen developed an amazingly simple and efficient system for keeping hand tools in order. They put up a sheet of "Peg Board" over the garage workbench, and hung tools off Peg Board hooks. To make things even easier, they traced around the tools, so they could quickly see if any tool was missing, what the tool was, and where it should be put back. This system still works wonders. Manufacturers have taken the idea one step further, creating custom perforated panels, with hanging pins specially made to support small tools, and special accessories such as hanging chisel trays and screwdriver racks. If

Traditional Peg Board panels are the time-tested and simple way to store tools out in the open so that you can see where everything goes, and know when a tool is missing. You might outline the tools, so you can tell at a glance exactly what goes where.

you're willing to pay the extra expense, consider this modern version. Otherwise, the old, basic Peg Board storage still does the trick. You can also keep tools in special hanging cabinets attached to wall studs, which lets you lock them up. Tool companies offer full lines of cabinets suited to many different types of tools. Although expensive, these are great places to store valuable collections of hand tools.

➤ BOX STORAGE: Every home should have a basic tool kit, including a set of Phillips and standard screwdrivers, a hammer, a tape measure, and other simple hand tools. Although you can hang all these, home projects are made much easier with a small, portable toolbox. The toolboxes come equipped with sturdy handles, and are increasingly made of lightweight but strong plastic construction. Plastic versions are usually less expensive than metal types. Look for

THE INSIDE SCOOP

STAGE CRAFT: Good work habits go hand in hand with the right storage space in keeping your tools organized. Borrow a strategy from professional contractors who use a site "stage." When you tackle a repair project, such as replacing a faucet, lay out all the tools you need on a clean rag before you start. Then put the tools back on the rag as soon as you are through using them. Once you're done with the job, it's easy to put all the tools back where they belong.

Special racks for individual power tools can keep them out of the reach of youngsters, and ready for use when you need them.

one with small utility drawers to hold a modest collection of screws, nails, and washers. A basic portable toolbox will be all most people need. But if your tool collection is more extensive, you need to consider a larger standing or rolling toolbox. Most of these are metal, and come with a variety of different depth drawers, attached cabinets, and open shelves. Choose the right type based on how many tools you need to store. An added advantage to standing or rolling tool chests is that the top can be an excellent work surface. Select a rolling toolbox for maximum flexibility in placement. The castors lock when the unit has to be stationary.

ZONE 3

Power Tools

🕐 30 MINUTES

Power tools represent a slightly different storage challenge than hand tools. They are bulkier and often come with a host of small accessory pieces that also must be organized. Older power tools were sold separate from accessories, with no containers for the tool itself. Today, most power tools come with carrying cases, and are often sold in complete sets with extra blades or bits contained in the same case as the power tool. Even if you have an older power tool, you can buy a carrying case to accommodate the tool and accessories—a great way to keep things organized. Store power tools adjacent to the hand tool zone, because power tools are often used in conjunction with hand tools. For safety—and because they are expensive—you may want to store power tools in a closed and locked cabinet. Dedicate different shelves in the cabinet to different types of tools, such as cutting, drilling, shaping, and so on. If your power tool has a

THE INSIDE SCOOP

RIGHT GUARD: Today's tools come with blade guards and safety blocks to prevent injury or damage when the tool isn't being used. Guards not only protect against injury, they also protect essential parts of the tool from damage. Regularly check your power tools to see that all guards are in place and in good working order, and replace those guards that are missing or damaged. Find replacement guards at large home centers or through manufacturers.

cord, use heavy-duty twist ties to keep the cord in a tidy loop. You can also opt to hang power tools that don't have their own cases. Buy a heavy-duty rack made specifically for this purpose, and hang the tools from their handles or body. Never hang a tool from its power cord; you can damage the cord and make the tool unsafe to use. If all your power tools are contained in their own cases, you can store them in a row on a sturdy, deep shelf. Position the shelf out of the reach of children.

ZONE 4

Yard and Garden Equipment and Supplies

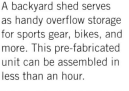 1 HOUR

Even a small yard with a couple of flower beds and borders requires a host of supplies and equipment. Basic lawn care can involve a mower, a gas can for the mower, a fertilizer spreader, bags of lawn food, and more. Keeping all this equipment in line makes the labor-intensive chore of yard care easier and more enjoyable. When organizing this zone, it's important to remember that everything must have a place of its own, and that different supplies and equipment in the zone be grouped according to purpose.

A backyard shed serves as handy overflow storage for sports gear, bikes, and more. This pre-fabricated unit can be assembled in less than an hour.

➤ **YARD-CARE POWER TOOLS:** Gas or electric yard tools can save hours of labor in the yard, but they need to be stored properly to remain in good working order, out of the way of traffic flow and out of the reach of children. If you have a lawn mower with a folding handle, always fold it up and position it as out of the way as possible. Lawn mower accessories

Above left: A standing organizer has slots for a variety of long-handled garden implements. The unit itself is durable and easily cleaned, and can be moved out of the garage right to where the work will be done.

such as a grass-catcher bag should be hung up, but cleaned out after every use to keep the mess out of your storage area. Lightweight tools such as weed trimmers, edgers, and hedge trimmers should be hung up as well. Keep fuel for gas-powered tools locked up in a metal cabinet to prevent accidents. Seasonal equipment such as snow blowers should be stored in a corner, out of the way of traffic flow in the garage. Always empty the fluids from seasonal equipment for off-season storage.

➤ LONG-HANDLED TOOLS: Rakes, shovels, hoes, and other long-handled yard tools are awkward to store. They should never just be left leaning against a wall or lying on a floor where they present safety hazards. Manufacturers provide a number of effective storage solutions for these implements. If you have the floor space, use a standing tool rack with separate cavities for each long-handled tool. More commonly, you'll find hanging racks with clip-in or slide-in handle holders, which will accommodate all kinds of tools, from spades with short, stocky handles to rakes with longer, thinner handles. Pick from simple hanging racks that support a few tools, or go for more complete structures with shelves, bins, and hose reels. No matter what type you buy, make sure it has the capacity to hold all your large, long-handled tools.

➤ SMALL GARDENING TOOLS: Smaller tools such as trowels and bulb-planting tools need to be kept tidy so they don't get misplaced. Hanging is a great way to store these, and many garden implements come

THE INSIDE SCOOP

HAMMER TIME: Nice as one looks, you don't necessarily need a special hanging organizer for your long-handled tools. If you're willing to go with a slightly cruder solution, hammer large penny nails into a wall or stud, leaving enough room for the tool handle between the nails. Hang the tool upside down between the nails so that it will be supported by its head.

CRAFTY CADDY: Bucket caddies are a wonderful way to keep your garden tools in order in a portable multipurpose organizer. The caddy is made of a tool belt wrapped around and attached to a 5-gallon plastic bucket. Take the tools and bucket wherever you go in your garden, and you'll have a place to put fresh-cut flowers, a handy hauler to move dirt from one place to the next, or a perfect place to toss weeds as you pull them.

STORAGE IN STYLE

POT O' TOOLS: Create attractive, inexpensive, and handy storage for small garden hand tools with the help of the most basic garden item—a terra-cotta or large, plastic plant-pot. Choose the size of pot that will accommodate all your hand tools, and stencil the word *tools* on the pot. Then place it on a shelf where you can get to the tools easily.

Opposite right: Keep your garden tools together in a rack designed for them. This wall-mounted unit is sturdy and easy to install.

Below left: The best way to keep any outdoor supplies in order is to dedicate a set of shelves to them. Here, a cleanable plastic shelving unit is used for a full complement of gardening supplies.

Below right: A durable garden shed nests in the corner of a deck and uses hangers and shelves to keep garden supplies and equipment in order.

with handle straps, holes, or rings so that they can be hung from pegs or hooks placed in a row. Even if the tools don't have straps, you can hang them on a small portion of Peg Board, with Peg Board hooks. High-end garden-tool sets come with their own durable storage cases, which let you keep all the tools together.

➤ **SUPPLIES:** The many supplies you use in landscaping your yard or maintaining your garden are the biggest storage challenge in a shed or garage. That's because they range in size and shape from small loose objects to oversized, hard-to-handle bags. Consequently, you need an array of storage solutions. Keep all your garden supplies together on a sturdy shelving unit.

Bagged supplies such as manure and lawn feed (and salt for the winter) can be stacked. But if your bags are prone to leakage, consider storing them in plastic tubs. Tubs are also a good idea for opened bags. If you don't use tubs, use plastic clips to keep opened bags from leaking.

Loose supplies such as flower-bed markers, fertilizer spikes, and seed packets are best kept in plastic boxes or trays on a shelf. Use a big enough container to ensure that the supplies are not jammed together. The containers should be labeled. Another option is to

STORAGE IN STYLE

ROUND AND ROUND: Garden hoses are a special storage challenge. Although they are brought inside in areas with freezing winters, during the rest of the year they are left outside. A disorganized hose is unsightly and can be just one more thing you can trip over or run over with the lawn mower. Fortunately, there are many organizers available to keep your garden hose under control. Long hoses that must reach far corners of the yard can be wound onto wheeled hose caddies that offer maximum mobility. Hose bowls—deep, decorative bowls that hold the wound-up hose—are more basic and attractive solutions. Metal hose reels are available in wall-mounted or stationary styles, and are easy to use.

hang an organizer comprised of canvas pockets (such as one used to organize shoes on the back of a door) on a wall stud or from the side of garage shelves. Group supplies by type in the different pockets.

Pots and planters should be stacked neatly and kept close to potting supplies. Keep plastic planters out of direct sunlight because too much exposure to direct sun can crack and fade unplanted plastic pots and boxes.

ZONE 5

Sports Gear

30 MINUTES

Devote a portion of the garage or shed to all your sports equipment. This way, you can relieve storage burdens from other parts of the house and collect all the gear in one place. Everyone will always know where to find the sports equipment, and where to put it back. When setting up this zone, make sure it covers all your sports, from a ball and hoop for the occasional game of one-on-one basketball to golf

Left: A wall-mounted sports rack keeps sporting equipment up off the floor and collected where it's easy to reach.

Center: Bikes can be in the way no matter where you put them, but mount them on the wall and they take up very little space.

Right: You can find specialized sporting goods racks for just about any sport. Here, tennis racquets are kept in order with a minimum of storage space.

A sporting goods rack can keep all the sports gear organized and ready for use—no matter their shapes and sizes. This durable rubber-and-plastic unit is sized just right to fit against the wall in a garage.

clubs, bikes, and more. Although you could cobble together a storage area with baskets, shelves, and cabinets, it's much wiser to buy custom racks meant for storing exactly the equipment you have. Sporting goods manufacturers make storage devices for just about any type of equipment.

➤ SKI AND/OR SNOWBOARD RACKS: You can buy individual hangers that keep snowboards or skis in place, but it usually makes more sense to purchase units integrated with shelving and hooks for boots and poles.

➤ BIKE-STORAGE SYSTEMS: The most basic types are coated wall hooks that support the frame of the bike. More advanced systems include bike trees that can store the bike horizontally or vertically, depending on available space. If you have lots of overhead clearance, consider a bike pulley system—the bike is mounted on suspended supports and then hoisted overhead and out of the way.

➤ FISHING-GEAR RACKS: These wire structures provide slots for several poles and plenty of space for a tackle box and a hanger for a net.

➤ MULTISPORT ORGANIZERS: These are a great choice if your family tends to play many different ball sports, such as baseball, tennis, and basketball, or if you have a lot of small accessories to store, such as knee pads and helmets for skateboarding. The organizer usually combines a large bin for loose balls and other items, hanging slots and hooks for bats and racquets, a shelf or small hangers for gloves, caps, and helmets, and additional storage accessories such as small bins.

THE INSIDE SCOOP

LOST AND NOT FOUND: The garage is a great place for a "last chance" carton or bin. Use a large carton and pitch into it everything that takes up space but isn't earning it: broken toys (no matter how cherished); outgrown books, clothing, games and puzzles; leftover tote bags and lunch boxes; and so on. If items have not been missed for a year, toss out the whole lot (after a quick check for anything worth passing along to a charity).

ZONE 6

Car Care

🕐 30 MINUTES

A cabinet that locks, such as this one, is a must for storing any hazardous materials such as gasoline or pesticides in the garage.

Decades ago when cars were mechanically simpler, you could save money by doing basic car repairs yourself. These days, most repairs relate to computerized functions within the car and are best left to professionals. But anyone who is willing to get his or her hands dirty can still save a little money by changing the oil, rotating tires, and performing other basic car maintenance. And most people like to keep their cars clean. The best way to keep car supplies organized is a sturdy set of shelves. Wire "restaurant shelving" can be most effective, but other shelf units can work as well, just as long as they are easily cleaned and have room for all your car supplies. To keep things simple, segregate supplies by function—keep extra oil and filters in one area, put all cleaning supplies on their own shelf, and so forth. Be sure to lock up these supplies to keep them away from curious children.

KEEPING UP

The exposed character of outbuildings and garages means that they are going to get dirty, and the rough nature of what they store means they may appear cluttered. That's why it's wise to give a shed or garage a thorough cleaning twice a year—once in the spring before spring planting and lawn mowing begin, and once in the fall as yard chores wind down. During these cleanings, remove everything from the space, sweep and clean it thoroughly, and then replace all your equipment and supplies. This will give you a chance to alter your organization as necessary, to check if any tools and equipment are damaged, and to find out if any bags or buckets of materials are leaking. Along with this biannual review, be sure to do the following:

• **BIN REVIEW:** Do a visual tour of the garage weekly, making sure that your recycling bins are not overfilled. If they are, replace them with larger, or more, bins.

• **THE MAINTENANCE MOMENT:** To keep your tools in good working order, regularly sharpen blades, clean moving parts, and lubricate mechanical pieces. Whenever you do this, make sure that your tools and equipment are stored where they won't be exposed to any kind of unusual wear.

CHAPTER 8

Foyers, Mudrooms, and Entryways

Entryways small and large are transitional areas where family members and visitors make the leap from outdoors to inside, often bringing coats and sweaters, packages, and other clutter in with them. Keeping entry areas clutter free means designing them for easy transitions, including elements that make it simple for everyone to see what should be left in the entryway (and where), and what should be brought into the house.

Your approach to clutter-proofing an entry room will vary depending on whether it is an informal entryway—the traditional "mudroom"—or a more formal foyer that is used by both family members and visitors. In many homes, these represent the rear-entry door and front door respectively. The times assigned to each zone are based on an average-sized space. If you have lots of children and visitors, you'll want to leave a little extra time to organize the zones.

Entryways are the most basic rooms in the home. Organizing them means focusing on the limited functions of the space. These are not general, long-term storage spaces, and should not be used to store files or papers, extra serving plates, or sports equipment.

Those items all have their places in other rooms. Entryways are only for those things that come off when you come into the house and go on when you leave.

Opposite: A well-ordered entryway has a place for anything that might be brought into the home.

STORAGE IN STYLE

FACE TIME: Children represent a challenge in keeping the entryway clutter free. To help young children consistently put their coats and other outerwear in the right spot, put a picture of each child over the hook, cubby, or shoe area he or she is supposed to use.

A single piece of furniture can help organize a small entryway, adding style as it brings order. This pretty hall bench "tree" is a perfect example of function and form.

A top shelf serves as a handy place for packages, attachés, and other items you want to remember to take with you on your way out the door.

A row of hooks provides accessible hanging storage for coats, scarves, handbags, and more. With the addition of a hanger, these can even be used for formal coats.

A tasteful umbrella stand provides all the room you'll need for canes and umbrellas.

Compartments under the bench can be left open to store footwear or, as shown here, to fill with wicker baskets that hold boots on one side, and mittens, gloves, and caps on the other.

ZONE 1

Coat Storage

15 MINUTES

Coats and jackets need to have a clear place to hang in the entryway so they don't clutter other rooms in the house. The two basic types of coats that need to be hung and organized are informal jackets that can be placed on hooks, and more upscale cold-weather garments that should be hung on hangers. When planning the coat storage you need, be sure to take into account the room you'll need for your family's outerwear and for visitors' coats. If you have the space, seasonal outerwear can be stored hung in the entryway. If the closet is too cramped, you'll need to store cold-weather garments during the spring and summer in the attic, or wherever you have extra closet space.

> ➤ COAT CLOSETS: The entryway closet should be dedicated to coats. Often, the closet will include a shelf. This should be used for other outerwear items, such as mittens and hats, as necessary. Equip entryway closets with a collection of sturdy hangers—wood or heavy-duty plastic are best; don't use metal hangers that will bend under the weight of clothes. The hangers should be able to support and maintain the bulky shape and weight of heavy winter coats, as well as lighter fall and spring wear. You can supply additional coat and sweater storage by attaching a rack with pegs or hooks to the back of the closet door. If small children are regulars in your entryway, make it easier for them to keep their coats organized by mounting a lower hanging bar in the closet. You can buy

A well-outfitted entry hall closet provides hanging space for long and short coats, and lots of shelves for hats, ponchos, and gloves.

A freestanding coat rack is an efficient way to accommodate coats, hats, scarves, and other garments. This version makes the most of limited space by including an umbrella stand as part of the base.

Opposite: One wall-mounted shelving unit can serve many purposes in the entryway. This one has ample shelf space on top, several sizeable compartments that can be assigned to different members of the family, and sturdy hooks for hanging garments.

a short hanging bar to suspend from the regular closet rod by hooks and chains. Wherever you store the coats, try to create a section for each person so that everyone in the house can quickly find his or her jackets and accessories when heading out the door.

➤ FREESTANDING OPTIONS: Many entryways don't have a closet, and even when they do, a freestanding piece of furniture can provide additional coat storage.

Coat racks are the simplest storage solution for entryways. Tall and thin, they fit well in confined spaces. Racks can hold several jackets and caps, although they can be unstable when burdened with heavy coats. They are best used as additions to closet space, or as the only coat storage in small households. The big advantage to a coat rack is its portability; it can be positioned in the handiest location, out of direct traffic flow. Some come equipped with umbrella stands integral to the base construction. Choose between metal or wood depending on which suits your entryway design best. If you have children, look for versions with midlevel hanging hooks in addition to the top "branches."

Hall trees are more complete storage solutions and better for busy households with many adults, children, and regular visitors. A hall tree is a single structure that includes a bench seat connected to a backboard, usually topped by a shelf, onto which hooks are fastened. Certain versions are made with a hanging rod that lets you suspend coats on hangers. Some come equipped with underbench shelves or cubbies, providing space off the floor for boots and shoes. Hall-tree benches are usually storage units themselves; the seat lifts up to reveal a chest space. This can be a handy location for scarves, mittens, umbrellas, and other inclement-weather gear.

Hooks and pegs give you the option of positioning hanging coat storage at eye level for the people in your household. Pegs are available in sets attached to a mounting base; buy individual hooks or hook sets as needed. Quick to install and inexpensive, these are especially handy for small children. Be sure to buy hooks meant for coats (they are longer and thicker). If this will be the primary way you store coats and jackets, be sure to install enough for both family members and visitors.

Footwear

🕐 15 MINUTES

Keeping boots, shoes, and other footwear in order goes a long way toward keeping your entryway clutter free. Stackable organizers are easy to clean and dividers keep each pair of shoes or boots in its own area.

Ironically, shoes are second only to toys as annoying underfoot clutter. The process of keeping shoes organized begins with providing enough space for all the footwear in your entryway. Shoes need to be kept either on a mat or on a movable supporting rack so that the floor underneath can be cleaned regularly. In a formal foyer, you can use mats placed inside the closet under the coats. In a less formal entryway or where there's no closet, use attractive wooden or metal shoe racks to hold shoes and boots, or use a dec-

orative wicker basket as an entryway accent and shoe organizer. Stackable shoe shelves are inexpensive and provide plenty of air circulation that will help wet shoes and boots to dry. No matter what you use to store shoes, it should be cleanable and able to catch dirt, salt, water, and so on. Keep shoes and boots in groups according to the person who wears them. If there is room, store boots in the entryway or foyer. If not, store them in the bedroom closet during the off season. Part of organizing the entryway should be removing the footwear that belongs somewhere else—basically any shoes or boots not specifically meant for inclement weather.

THE INSIDE SCOOP

SOCK HOP: Increasingly, American households are adopting the Asian practice of removing shoes in the entryway, before entering the house proper. Although this may seem a bit odd to people who are used to keeping their shoes on unless they are sleeping, there is a good reason to go shoeless in the home. The soles of most shoes track in dirt and allergens such as pollen. Those indoor pollutants can then get ground into rugs as people walk around the home, creating an unhealthy situation. To keep your home as pollutant-free as possible, provide an entryway rack or space where family members and visitors can put their shoes.

Mail and Keys

30 MINUTES

Although you usually deal with both keys and mail in the entryway, keys seem to disappear when you need them, while bills seem to accumulate when you don't. Both problems are addressed with similar solutions—a specific place for them in the entryway.

➤ **KEYS:** Keep your keys from getting lost by giving them a specific place where they go the minute you walk in the door. You can use any of a number of key hangers available in a diversity of styles. You can also go the less expensive route of just mounting a hook for the keys on a wall or other nearby surface. If you have multiple sets of keys—including backup sets of your house keys and keys to locked sheds, second or third cars, and relatives' houses—keep them all in the same place. You may be reluctant to put anything more on the walls, especially if a key hanger interferes with your decor. In that case, keep keys in a decorative bowl or similar shallow container on a table by the door.

➤ **MAIL:** Ideally, you would bring your mail in and take it right to where it should go—bills to the home office, catalogs to the bedroom or the living room, junk mail to the recycling bin or garbage. But, in reality, few people want to deal with mail the first thing on entering their home. That's not a problem if you take a little time to set up a mail station in the entryway. If you have open wall space, mount wood or metal wall files like those used for magazines, or hang a decorative fabric pouch. If you have a table in your entryway, use trays or bins to keep mail tidy. Whatever storage solution you use, keep it out in the open so that you'll see when you have a backlog of mail and be more likely to deal with it.

An attractive, wall-mounted organizer keeps mail—from letters to flyers—right where you can find it. Key hooks make finding your keys an easy chore.

Seasonal Storage

🕐 30 MINUTES

Seasonal items are all those things that get used specifically for different times of the year. These include umbrellas, mittens and gloves, hats and scarves, and gardening clogs and kneepads. For busy households and large families, a multibin organizer can keep the entryway in order. Each member of the family gets a bin for his or her own caps, hats, mittens, and other foul-weather gear.

➤ UMBRELLAS: Umbrellas should be stored standing up. When laid on their side, the ribs can get damaged. The best umbrella stands allow for air circulation around the umbrellas so that they can dry effectively when brought in out of the rain. This doesn't mean you have to go in search of an actual umbrella stand. Wicker or wire-mesh trash baskets can function perfectly well as umbrella holders.

➤ SCARVES, MITTENS, AND GLOVES: Scarves are generally hung up to make them accessible and to air them out. But they can be

KEEPING UP

With enough hooks and other storage, entryways should stay orderly on their own because nobody spends much time there. But you still need to check the area periodically to keep it clutter free.

• COAT CHECK: Every week, make sure coats are hung in their proper places. Rehang those that have fallen off their hooks or hangers, and put coats that have migrated to someone else's section of the closet back where they belong. When seasons change, make sure that you move heavy jackets and boots to seasonal storage.

• DISORDERLY CONDUCT: Every two or three days, check on the orderliness of shoes and boots in the closet. Rearrange them if necessary so that they are easily accessible when needed.

• MAIL CALL: If you've equipped the foyer or entryway with a mail receptacle, perform a Saturday morning check to see that nothing important has been left in the receptacle, and that mail is being moved to where it needs to go.

Opposite: A variety of hanging storage ensures that this entryway can accommodate many visitors and coats short and long. The wall hooks are great for informal jackets and scarves, and a box on the top shelf keeps mittens and gloves in order.

An umbrella stand does not need to be a conventional metal type. Here, a wooden bucket holds umbrellas and canes in a unique country style.

folded and stored in bins or baskets in the closet or on shelves or in cubbies in the entryway. Mittens and gloves need to be kept with their mates, and should be kept in storage that allows for air to circulate around them. A shallow woven or mesh tray or basket is ideal. If many people are using the entryway, consider including several clothespins in mitten and glove storage, so that mates can be pinned together.

➤ **GARDENING GEAR:** If you are an avid gardener and like to put your garden togs on as you go out the door, the mudroom is a logical place to keep your favorite gardening shirt, clogs, kneepads, and apron. Garden footwear should be kept on a simple shoe rack that is easy to clean. Other gardening apparel can be kept in a bin or attractive basket on a shelf or on the floor by the back door.

CHAPTER 9

Home Offices and Work Spaces

These days, the term "home office" covers many different work spaces, from well-equipped rooms used by people who telecommute or work at home full time to compact corners or nooks where people pay bills, review paperwork, and conduct the business of keeping a household. If you're lucky, you have a whole room to dedicate to your home office. More likely, you'll have to make do with a smaller space.

That's not to say you have to work in messy quarters or deal with constant clutter. A small home office can function every bit as well as one that takes up a large room, as long as it is thoughtfully designed. It is a matter of necessity meeting imagination. Your home office may be a rolltop desk painted the same colors as your kitchen and tucked into a corner by the pantry. It might take up an alcove off a living room, or be crafted from a portion of a large entryway that you partition off with a decorative screen or rolling bookshelves. When it comes to beating clutter, the way you set up your home office is more important than the amount of square footage you have.

The organizational challenge of a home office is twofold: keeping household clutter from invading the workspace, and keeping work items from cluttering other areas in the house. In both cases, loose papers are your enemy. That's why the first rule of home offices is to organize papers—in a file cabinet or on some sort of display organizer like a bulletin board—or toss them.

If you have a bulletin board, keep it organized. Avoid bulletin-board clutter by not overlapping papers you hang up, by promptly

Opposite: Nestled in the corner of a room, this work space is a fully functional office with lots of storage.

A well-appointed office makes good use of small organizers that work with the wealth of concealed storage space.

Magazine cases are a great way to keep magazines, catalogs, manuals, and other reference materials organized and easy to find.

A mix of drawers and cabinets ensures that work items small and large have a place to go.

A quartet of wire in-trays keeps paperwork in order and holds a supply of fresh paper for printing and notetaking.

Wide "lateral" filing cabinets are built into the underdesk area, optimizing available space. No extra stand-alone cabinets are needed.

A fire-safe lockbox is a good addition to any office, as a place to keep important one-of-a-kind documents and other valuables that would be difficult, if not impossible, to replace.

taking down notices and other materials that are out of date, and by removing papers that should be filed. Group similar papers together on the bulletin board to make them easier to find, and always hang papers as level as possible to make them easy to read at a glance.

Of course, keeping papers in control is only part of the battle. You also want an office layout and accessories that make work easier, more efficient, and more comfortable, and where you can quickly find what you need. That's why your choices of a desk, reference storage, file organization, and technology are crucial. (If you rely heavily on a great deal of computer equipment in your office, assume that Zone 2, "Technology and Equipment," will take you extra time.) Choose wisely, and you'll end up with a tidy and attractive work area that promotes productivity.

ZONE 1
Desk

🕐 15 MINUTES

The desk is the center of the home office. Many people adapt an existing extra table or desk to the purpose. But the important role the desk plays makes choosing the right one essential to beating clutter. First and foremost, your desk must be the right size for your needs. A desk that is too small makes it hard to work efficiently and keep the basic office tools at hand. But a desk that is too large becomes a wide, empty space inviting clutter. Remember, too, that permanently organizing your desk means setting up the desktop to facilitate work, not clutter, and optimizing underdesk storage when you can.

➤ **DESKTOP:** Your desktop should provide enough room for basic office tools and for space to comfortably write, to open your mail, and to review files as necessary. There should be enough room around everything to

Opposite: Sometimes a home office will be used only as a place to pay bills and answer e-mail. This alcove off a kitchen supplies all the room necessary for an occasional work space.

THE INSIDE SCOOP

FIND A FOLDER: A basic folder portfolio with room for a writing tablet and a pocket for loose papers can serve as the perfect home office assistant. Use the writing paper to record notes on phone calls or to jot down a quick to-do list. The place for papers should be large enough to hold several ready-to-be-filed papers, but not so large as to let you fall way behind on your filing.

DOLLAR SMART

OFFICE DOOR: Why pay a king's ransom for a large, stylish desk when you can make your own customized version for a lot less? Buy a hollow-core door, paint it your favorite color, and set it on two sawhorses painted a contrasting color for a stunning office focal point. Or lay the door across two half-height file cabinets to efficiently incorporate function with form.

STORAGE IN STYLE

AIR PLAY: When desk space is at a premium, look for solutions out of thin air—hang bins and trays over the desk. Shop for organizing systems that clip onto the back edge or side of the desk and suspend trays, pen cups, and other accessories over the desk surface, leaving you plenty of space for your paperwork and files underneath. Be sure to leave room for your work space.

allow movement—so you don't bump your computer monitor while reaching for a pencil. In figuring out how big your desk needs to be, you should work with the other zones of the home office. For instance, you may prefer to use a desktop wire file-organizer for often-needed files. But if the home-office space will not accommodate a large desk, those files are better placed in the front of your file cabinet or in a drawer. In most home offices, the computer monitor, keyboard, and mouse form the central grouping of the desk, with other essentials positioned around this group. When setting up or reorganizing your desk, focus on the essentials. If you have extra room, it's okay to add a picture or two to your desktop arrangement. But don't go crazy with decorative paperweights or funny novelty statues.

Basic desktop implements such as pen and pencil holders, stapler, and tape dispenser should be grouped together. The best way to do this is to use an all-in-one organizer. These are available as stepped racks or as carousels. You can buy complete plastic or wood organizers with matching stapler, scissors, pencil sharpener, ruler, letter opener, staple remover, and tape dispenser.

In- and out-boxes are timeless organizing tools that no desk should be without. These can be wire, steel, plastic, or wood trays that are part of coordinated desk sets. You can also use decorative lacquered trays or other flat, shallow containers to suit your own tastes.

A mail organizer is also essential because the home office is the natural location for dealing with bills, direct-mail offers, catalogs, and other mail.

A mix of cabinets and shelves allows the user to keep vital supplies and often-used materials in plain view, while concealing backup items and less frequently used files.

Select from any number of slotted mail organizers to keep incoming and outgoing mail in order. Many of these can organize mail by date or subject, and some come with drawers underneath for envelopes, stamps, and other mail-related supplies.

➤ DRAWERS AND UNDERDESK STORAGE: Traditional desks with drawers provide additional storage for things you would prefer to keep out of view. But the problem with drawers is precisely that everything is hidden. It's easy to put things there without thinking, and the drawers can quickly turn into clutter buckets. To make best use of your drawers and keep them as organized as possible, commit each drawer to one type of storage, and partition drawers as necessary to keep things

THE INSIDE SCOOP

SHINE ON: Desktop space is too valuable to waste on large lighting fixtures. Look to save space with the home-office lighting you choose. Select adjustable desktop lamps with bases that are heavy enough to prevent tipping and thin bodies and necks that can focus the light exactly where you need it—and be swung out of the way when necessary. If you prefer a fixed lamp, make sure the body is narrow and the bulb and lamp shade are as small as possible while still providing the illumination you need.

Above left: Where space or expense is an issue, you may not want to install cabinets or shelves. In that case, opt for desktop organizers such as these stackable units, with compartments that keep supplies neat and accessible.

Above right: A month's worth of slots and two drawers make this mail organizer an excellent tool for keeping bills and other mail under control. Any good mail organizer should let you see individual envelopes, rather than stacks of them.

neat. For instance, use your top drawer to hold pens in a plastic drawer organizer and to stack writing tablets and paper for the printer. Even when the desk does not have drawers, the underdesk area can still be used for storage and organization. Keyboard trays attached to the underside of the desk give you a place to put your keyboard while keeping desk space free. When you are not using the computer, the keyboard slips underneath, out of sight. You can use the space where a row of drawers would normally be for rolling storage, such as a rolling file cabinet or a low, rolling printer stand.

ZONE 2

Technology and Equipment

30 MINUTES

Today's home office is usually equipped with some measure of technology, even if it's just an old computer and hand-me-down printer. The cords, peripherals, and odds and ends that go along with even a modest home-office setup are a big organizational challenge. The good news is that new technological advances, such as wireless technology, can help you beat clutter.

THE INSIDE SCOOP

PAPERLESS POSSIBILITIES: Your computer isn't just an organizational lifesaver in the home office; it can also be a clutter solution. Many people don't realize that today's computers come equipped with programs that can replace a lot of the paper that clutters a home office. For instance, most modern computer systems have simple address-book programs built into the computer's basic operating system. Even if yours doesn't, you can choose from among many inexpensive software packages available to manage lists of contacts, day-to-day calendars, checking and savings accounts, and more. Use your computer to capacity and you can toss your address book, calendar, and a host of other paper files. If you feel uncertain about going paperless, then back up your data on a regular basis and keep a hard copy of all important items.

➤ **COMPUTERS:** Making space for your computer is often the first step in setting up a home office. If you are one of the increasing number of people choosing to use a laptop as your personal computer, the space you'll need is modest—just a square foot or so of desktop space. If you have a more traditional desktop system, with a separate monitor, CPU (computer processing unit, which is the body of the computer), keyboard, and mouse (or if you use a separate monitor and keyboard to make working with your laptop easier), you need more room.

The CPU is one of two types: a contemporary vertical "tower" or the traditional horizontal "desktop" version. Towers can be placed on top of the desk, but taller ones tend to look awkward there and are often best stored under the desk. Make it easier to move the computer CPU for cleaning or dealing with cords by mounting the CPU on a CPU stand or a wheeled trolley. Or buy computer hangers that mount to the underside of the desk and hold the CPU up off the floor. Desktop-computer CPUs can often support a small monitor placed on top. If you think the monitor is too heavy, buy a monitor stand big enough to allow the CPU to slide underneath.

The monitor can be a big space hog on your desk. But it doesn't have to be. If it's time to update your equipment, consider buying a flat-panel monitor. These screens take up very little room and can provide the same or better graphics quality as large, boxy desktop versions. If you have a traditional monitor, make the most of desk space by placing it on a monitor stand so that the space underneath it is still usable.

➤ **CORDS:** The various cords needed to connect different devices to each other and to a power source too often

Free up desktop space and keep your computer tower safe from getting knocked over by using an underdesk hanger. Hanging the tower also makes for easier floor cleaning.

When considering a home office desk, look for cord slots that keep cables and cords organized and out of your way.

create an unsightly, dirt-collecting, disorderly mess. There are two basic options for keeping this particular clutter culprit in check: Keep all cords together, or do without them entirely. These strategies apply to all types of cords that transfer data to and between equipment, including DSL, cable, and USB cords.

Capture your cords with a cord organizer. There are two types: flexible tubes that keep the cords concealed so you can run a bundle of cords wherever they need to go and rigid cord "channels" that also contain all your cords in one outer shell. Although less flexible, the channels are more easily attached to surfaces such as the underside of your desk or wall baseboards. Lengths of rigid channels are put together by combining sections of straight pieces and corner "elbows." Both flexible and rigid organizers are available in a wide selection of colors, finishes, and materials. You can also choose from simple, less-expensive plastic braces with clip-in slots for cables and wires. One is positioned about every foot to keep the cords and wires untangled and running parallel for their length.

Go wireless for a streamlined, more complete solution. Many of today's computers, peripherals, and input devices (keyboards and mice) offer wireless models and solutions. For building wireless home networks, Wi-Fi is the protocol. This technology lets you surf the Web, share files between computers, and even print—all without wires. For mice, keyboards, and printers, infrared or Bluetooth technology can be used to eliminate the wires between peripherals and the PC.

➤ DIGITAL CAMERAS AND MUSIC PLAYERS: Today's computers let you download music and upload images from digital cameras to your computer. New computers have special ports for cables that connect the music player or camera to the computer. When you are not downloading

THE INSIDE SCOOP

SCREENING ROOM: Desktop cramped for space? Make use of the sides of your computer monitor with a monitor-top organizer. Made in different sizes, these organizers fit across the top of the monitor and have pockets hanging on each side. The pockets can be used to hold small items such as pens, stamps, and so on. These organizers don't work on flat-screen monitors.

TIED UP: Turn to your local home center or hardware store for an inexpensive and effective cord organization solution. Industrial connector ties—professional versions of the twist ties you use for garbage bags—are easy to use and can keep a group of cables or wires bundled securely together.

A handsome rolling organizer keeps supplies handy in the top drawer and hanging files organized in the bottom drawer.

Opposite: Small home offices can benefit from space-saving specialty furniture. Here, a printer drawer keeps cords and cables in check and hides the printer when not in use.

or uploading, store the camera and music player in an appropriate area away from the home office so that they don't clutter the desktop and risk getting broken. A digital camera can be stored in a box or in its own case along with your other photographic equipment or photos. If you tend to use the music player when you go out, keep it where you store your wallet and other valuables. Otherwise, store it in a drawer or other safe place.

➤ **PRINTER:** Although high-quality printers have gotten smaller over time, they still take up an inordinate amount of surface area. Sophisticated laser printers are self-contained but are generally large. More common ink-jet printers are smaller, but need space for the paper feed and the paper output, increasing their "footprint" on the desktop or shelf. You also need room to remove or insert paper and replace ink cartridges, further complicating printer placement. You can make efficient use of desktop space by placing a printer on a desktop printer stand. Available in clear acrylic, colored plastic, metal, or wood, printer stands range from simple platforms that create an empty storage space underneath to more complex workstations with multiple drawers, cord channels, shelves, and other features. Of course, if your home office has the floor space, you can place the printer on an independent printer stand, with room for reams of paper, supplies, and more. You can even buy a mobile workstation with room for other devices, such as a fax and a scanner. Just be aware that cords will limit how mobile the station can be.

➤ **SCANNER:** Today's home computer stations often include a scanner that lets you scan and send photos to friends or scan art for party invitations, holiday greeting cards, personal newsletters, and more. Where you place your scanner depends on how often you use it, how much desk space you have, and the length of its cables. If you tend to use it only once a month,

STORAGE IN STYLE

WALLET WATCH: Software CDs and DVDs and backup disks can take up a significant amount of shelf space when stored in their protective jewel cases. Condense computer disks into one manageable unit with a CD wallet. Many organizers come in fabric, leather, and vinyl, and have individual sleeves for CDs and a zipper to keep out dust and dirt.

you might want to keep the scanner on a shelf, moving it to the desk when you use it. If you use it more often, find space for the scanner on your desk, or use a desktop printer stand so that you still have room beneath the scanner.

➤ TELEPHONE, ANSWERING MACHINE, AND FAX: Essential communication devices play a key role in the home office. Although you may not have a fax, chances are you have a phone and an answering machine. The answering machine is usually located with the phone (or as part of the base station of a cordless phone), so the two form a unit. If you work at home full-time, you should look into adding a voice-mail option to your phone services. This option lets you eliminate a physical answering machine and receive messages while you are on the phone.

Phones don't have to take up a lot of room in the home office. Most phones come with brackets that allow them to be mounted on the wall. You may prefer to use a cordless phone and keep the base station in another room, closer to an installed phone jack. If you use a headset when working in your home office, be sure that it has a place to go when you're not using it, such as a hook or a desktop cradle.

Traditional fax machines present the same organizational challenges that printers do. Not only do you need to make room for the fax machine itself, you also need room for paper supply and output. In addition, the fax machine will need to be connected to a phone line that has to be run from the nearest phone jack. That's why the best option is often a computer "on-board" fax system. You can buy computer software that will let you fax documents directly from your computer to an outside number, through your Internet service. The drawback of this technique is that you can't fax existing paper documents. But if you have a scanner, you can scan documents into the computer and then fax them.

A dedicated printer stand such as this keeps all printed documents and printer supplies in order. A wheeled unit allows you to move the printer out of the way when not in use.

THE INSIDE SCOOP

PRINTER HIDEAWAY: If you have a large desk with lots of room underneath, consider a rolling printer stand. It is short enough to fit right under the desk, and usually comes with an additional shelf for paper or other supplies. When you need to print a document, just pull the printer out from under the desk.

RUNNING INTERFERENCE: Be aware that wireless devices and home networks can be disrupted by the signals of cordless phones operating at certain frequencies (microwave ovens may also cause disruption). If you are experiencing problems with wireless accessories, temporarily replace your cordless phone with a traditional unit to test if the phone is the problem.

➤ **COPIERS AND MULTIPURPOSE UNITS:** If you regularly use a copier in your home office, or have a multipurpose machine (one that includes a variety of functions, such as copying, faxing, and scanning), set up a dedicated station for it. The unit can sit atop a stationary cabinet or a cart with wheels, but the support structure should have enough room underneath for extra paper, replacement ink and cartridges, scanner bulbs, and other replacement supplies. The top surface of the cart or cabinet should have room for the copier or combination unit and a tray to hold copies that need to be made, faxes that have just come in, and other documents.

ZONE 3

Supplies and Reference Storage

⚙ 1 HOUR

Whether you're using a home office for writing a novel, running a real estate business, or just trying to keep bills straight and the household running, you'll need space for supplies and reference materials. In some cases, you'll have to store books that you use in your professional role. You may need a place to keep cooking magazines with recipes you want to try in the future. And no matter what you're planning to do in your home office, you'll need supplies such as printer paper, staples, tape, and other basics. In most home offices, shelves are the best option for storing supplies and reference materials. Open storage lets you see what you have and what you need, and find books, magazines, and manuals without searching high and low. You can choose between stand-alone shelf units and wall-mounted shelves. Make your decision based on how much shelf space you need, your available office space, and what you need to store. For instance, if you need to store only a few magazines and some office supplies, a wall-mounted shelf may offer all the space and stability necessary. But if you have more floor space and need to store multiple reams of paper and thick reference books, you'll probably want to use a self-standing bookshelf.

Paper and stationery supplies such as envelopes are best kept neatly stacked on shelves. Keep them away from any water sources such as a fish tank or water cooler and heat sources such as a radiator or space heater. Store reams of papers on their edges, by type (for example, regular paper, photo-grade paper, and three-hole paper). If you don't have a bookend or other firm support on the shelf next to the paper, keep the different papers in file folders.

Magazines are best kept orderly in magazine racks. These standing boxes have cutouts that let you see the spines of the magazines and easily grab any individual issue. Stacked piles of magazines have a tendency to become disorganized, as the slippery gloss covers slide against one another. Stacking also makes it more difficult to pull out magazines at the bottom of the pile.

Books should be grouped by type so you can easily and quickly find the reference you need at any given time. Heavier books, such as large dictionaries, should be kept on lower shelves to prevent standing shelves from tipping and attached shelves from pulling away from the wall. Use bookends rather than books stacked on their sides at the end of a row; stacked books are more difficult to pull out.

Office supplies come in all sizes and shapes, from individual pens to boxes of staples to loose rolls of tape. To accommodate the variety, keep office supplies in a dedicated box or bin on the shelf, or in drawers by type of supply.

Below: Fax machines, copiers, scanners, and other stand alone devices should have their own place. This fax stand has room for replacement supplies, paper, and incoming fax files.

Opposite: Make the best use of office shelves by placing labeled boxes to hold supplies, files, and reference materials on them. This office also has a prefabicated organizer unit with space for a printer, hanging files, and slide-out bins in a range of sizes.

ZONE 4

Files

1 HOUR

One of the biggest challenges in keeping your home office in order is your filing system. Home-office files can quickly become disorganized without you realizing it. Sometimes you may put files back out of order because you are in a hurry. Occasionally you may not be able to locate a new file folder, so you just place a piece of paper wherever it fits. Whatever the case, take this opportunity to review and revise your filing system to ensure it is as logical and easy to use as possible. Start by reviewing all your paper files. Throw out what you no longer need and move files such as old tax returns to long-term storage in the attic or garage. Once you've pared down your files to what you absolutely need to store, plan your filing system.

THE FILE QUESTIONS

The best way to organize your files well is to answer three basic questions.

1. **Do your files have a system?** You should be able to concisely explain how your filing system works, and finding a file should be simple and intuitive—so that even someone who has never worked with your system could figure it out. If not, you need to refine your system. One of the best filing methods is a simple alphabetic system organized by the first letter of the topic. You also want to keep the file papers in order, so that any single file is organized from newest papers in front to the oldest in back, or vice versa.

2. **Do you have enough space for your files?** If you are cramming files into an overstuffed cabinet, you may be tempted to throw away essential files, and you will have trouble accessing the files you need. Do a realistic assessment of your file-storage needs and add another cabinet if you need it.

3. **Can you computerize some of your paper files?** These days, much of what we formerly retained and stored as paper can be converted to computer files. Taxes and banking can be done online and stored on a disk, copies of correspondence can be kept on your hard drive, and product information you might once have stored for future reference is now often available at companies' Web sites or as software supplied with electronic products. Computerizing paper files can make organizing them an easier task, and makes for less paper clutter. Make sure you keep a hard (paper) copy of vital records and documents, though.

Shelving keeps reference materials in order in this streamlined, minimalist home work space.

Take a few minutes to map out on a piece of paper the titles of the hanging file folders in your cabinet, and the files within those hanging folders. This exercise will reveal any flaws in your filing system and let you correct them quickly, with little effort. Once you have planned the order of your files, reorganize them within the file cabinet. Of course, the cabinet you use will depend on the space in your home office and the way you prefer to work. File cabinets come in diverse shapes and sizes, from half-height, two-drawer units to tall, wide lateral-file cabinets. You'll find file cabinets and cases in wood, metal, plastic, and more unusual combinations, such as fabric or wicker around a steel-wire frame.

➤ ROLLING FILES: Rolling file cabinets can be quite handy for the home office, letting you easily move the files around in the space as your needs change. Rolling cabinets are limited to two-drawer, half-height models; taller four-drawer units would be prone to tipping over if placed on casters. The simplest version of a mobile filing unit is the trolley, an open frame with wheels. The files hang from fixed runners along the top of the frame. Some have two levels, but this feature only increases the natural instability of these types of units. Not only are they more likely to tip over than solid-sided cabinets, the framework lets file folders slip

STORAGE IN STYLE

HUE VIEW: The traditional beige manila file folder has given way to a spectrum of file-folder options. This provides the opportunity for you to color-code files. Use blue for personal files and red for business files, or create your own rainbow-colored organization scheme. The results will be as much office flair as file system.

THE INSIDE SCOOP

FLAME FREE: Every home office can benefit from a fireproof safe. Use the safe for extremely important documents such as birth certificates and essential letters that exist only in paper form. Find affordable fireproof safes at home centers, hardware stores, and large discount retailers. Put the safe in an inconspicuous location, but one that you can easily access when necessary.

Double-width underdesk file cabinet drawers are a good alternative to a separate file cabinet.

out of the sides of hanging folders. Consequently, if you choose a trolley-type cabinet, pick one with solid sides.

➤ STATIONARY CABINETS: File cabinets that sit flat on the floor are the more traditional home office choice. The two types are lateral and vertical. Files in lateral cabinets hang so that they face the sides of the wide cabinets. Vertical file cabinets are more common in home offices—the files are arranged front to back in the cabinet. Stationary cabinets are usually more stable than wheeled units, especially when the cabinet is loaded with files; the weight transfer when a file drawer is opened or closed is more evenly distributed in a stationary cabinet than it would be with wheels.

KEEPING UP

Home offices need to be regularly monitored to ensure that clutter is not getting in the way of productivity. Periodic spot checks help you stay ahead of clutter and keep the office as organized as possible.

• **The telltale snapshot:** Once each week, walk into your work space, stop, and take a mental snapshot of your desk. Are papers strewn about? Are computer disks creating a messy pile? Is your desktop pen carousel empty because pens have been taken out and not returned? Put the desk back in order, paying special attention to any papers or items that don't have a logical place to go. Buy new organizational aids as needed to refine your work space and accommodate the way you work, and take a few minutes to return everything to its rightful place so that you can work with a clear space and mind.

• **Shelf shuffle:** Every 2 weeks, check your shelf inventory of supplies, and order paper, ink cartridges, computer disks or CDs, and anything else you need. The beauty of an organized shelf is that you can see right away when you're low on necessities.

• **Filed down:** Every 6 months, go through your files to determine if any are no longer in use and should be archived. Check that files are not crammed into the file cabinet. If they are, buy another file cabinet. During this review, go through your files and make sure they are logically organized so that everything is easy to find. Disorderly files lead to paper clutter when you're not sure where a document should be filed.

CHAPTER 10

Laundry Rooms

Laundry room location is dictated by power and water lines and the venting necessary for a dryer to operate. This means that sometimes the laundry room may not be a room at all; it might be a corner of the basement or an alcove off the kitchen. It may even be located in the garage. But no matter where your laundry room is situated, the chosen area should provide clearance enough to maneuver around the washer and dryer, adequate storage for laundry supplies, and, ideally, a place to fold and iron clothes.

The organizational challenge in a laundry room is to set it up so that what you do there can be done efficiently. Everything in a laundry room should have a place to go when not in use. For instance, if you leave your ironing board out at all times, it will become a parking place for a wide array of clutter. Without an established folding area, newly dried clothes tend to migrate all over the laundry room—and beyond. Fortunately, the laundry room is focused on function. The only purposes you need to account for are washing, drying, folding, and ironing clothes.

ZONE 1

Supplies Storage

⏱ 30 MINUTES

Storage for laundry-room supplies need not be extensive because there is only so much you'll need to store. However, if you are looking to buy laundry supplies in bulk, consider a complete laundry-center unit. These bracket the washer and dryer with shelves and cabinets and can often supply the storage space you need for cleaning supplies, baskets to organize clothes for washing and folding, and more. In many cases, a more modest amount of storage will be sufficient. You can opt for cabinets or shelving—whichever suits the space and your preferences.

Opposite: Storage is style in this chic laundry room that brings shelves, baskets, a tall laundry cart, and a hanging rod together to create a highly efficient space.

A neat laundry room combines different types of storage to serve a multitude of needs.

Cabinets with safety latches keep detergents and other hazardous materials away from children.

Open shelving can be used for frequently needed items, or for small loose supplies.

A rod positioned over the sink lets you hang ironed items, or hang garments to drip dry.

A tall cabinet stores the ironing board and some large cleaning supplies such as brooms and mops.

A wall-mounted unit offers a stable surface for folding clothes, and bins to hold folded items. The pull-out bins can be removed to carry clean clothing.

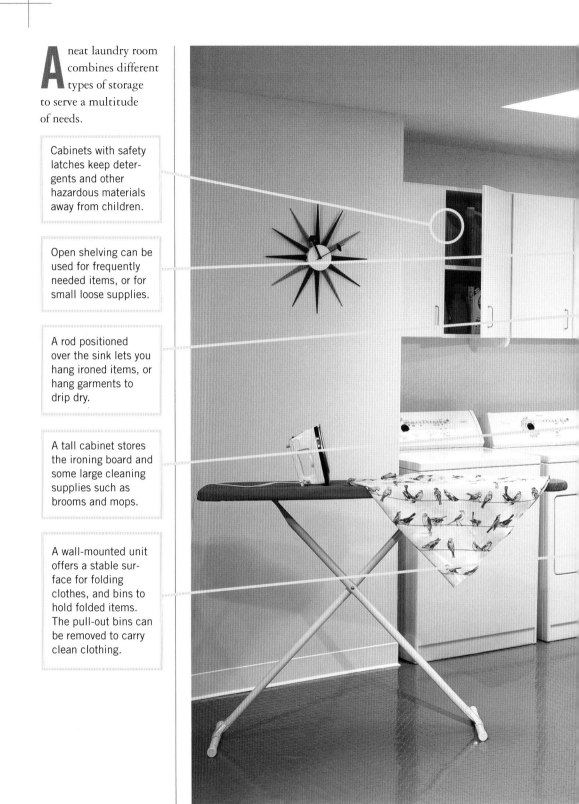

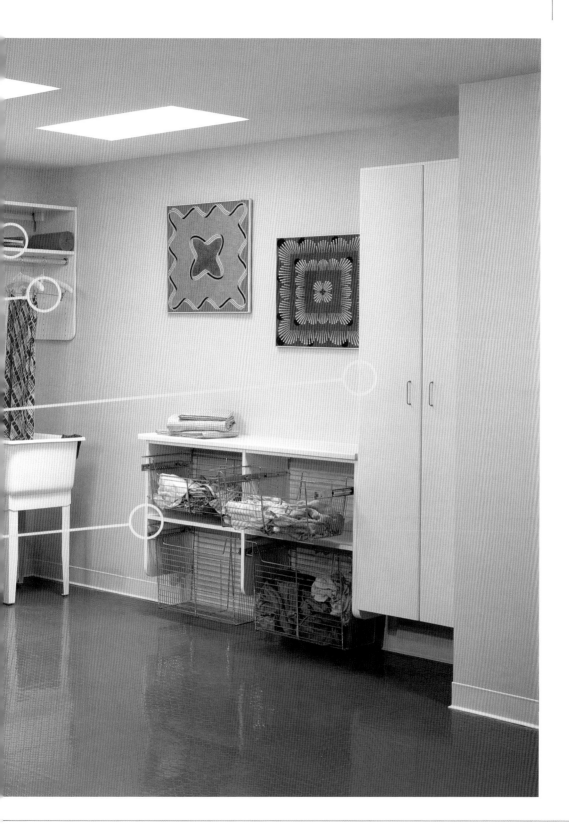

STORAGE IN STYLE

MAGNETIC PERSONALITY: Keep small supplies you use most often—like boxes of dryer sheets, stain remover, and other fairly light bottles or boxes—close at hand with a magnetic organizer hung on the side of your washing machine. These are available as simple net bags with magnetic hangers or sturdier plastic bins with stronger magnetic attachments.

THE INSIDE SCOOP

PORTABLE PLACES: In some situations, such as garages with cement walls, hanging cabinets or shelves will be very difficult, if not impossible, to install. That doesn't mean you have to do without effective storage. You can find independent laundry-room carts and shelf stands at bed and bath shops and home centers. Some are thin shelving units that fit neatly in the confined space between the washer or dryer and adjacent walls. For convenient storage, choose a trolley unit that can be wheeled where you need it and then out of the way when the laundry is done.

Opposite top: Wall-mounted prefabicated cabinets supply a large amount of varied storage. Short and tall cabinets ensure that everything from spray starch to a collapsible folding table can be stored away. The hanging organizer inside the tall cabinet door keeps the dust mop out of the way, but ready for use.

Opposite left: A wire shelf unit stands over the washer and dryer and supports folded items. The fold-out arm accommodates hanging clothes.

Opposite right: This organizer hangs on the back of a closet door, storing as many supplies as a large cabinet could.

Shelves are generally less expensive and easier to put up. Whichever type of storage you choose to use, the key is to position the storage above or close to the washer and dryer, where the supplies will be used.

➤ **LAUNDRY SUPPLIES:** Whether you use cabinets or shelves, keep supplies separated by type, using organizers for groups of smaller items. For instance, keep bleach, fabric softener, and detergent together, stain and spot removers and stain pretreatments in their own tray, and so on. To make things even easier, keep your supplies in order of use near where you use them, with detergent, bleach, and fabric softener organized in that order near the washing machine, and dryer sheets kept near the dryer. Consider washer and dryer pedestals with storage drawers. Your washer or dryer is placed on the pedestal, which not only gives you storage space in the drawer, but also raises the height of the unit, reducing your need to bend to do laundry. However, if there are children in your home, dangerous supplies such as bleach must go on shelves or cabinets well out of their reach, or in locked cabinets next to the washer or dryer.

➤ **LAUNDRY:** You won't always be able to wash dirty clothes the minute you bring them into the laundry room, so you'll need to make room near the washer for "incoming" loads. You may need more than one laundry basket if you have a large family or you want to presort. If you presort your clothes before washing, use hampers to make the process easier. Three simple canvas or mesh baskets on a shelf—for bright colors, darks, and whites—can help you keep dirty laundry organized for washing, keep the clothes off the floor, and make sure that dirty clothes never find their way into piles of clean laundry waiting to be folded. You can buy manufactured laundry-sorter units comprised of three mesh or fabric bags in a single chrome or wood frame.

Ironing Station

⏱ 30 MINUTES

Below left: This combination ironing board and laundry cart makes the most of any space. The mesh bag compartments can be used for ironed folded items, or to separate laundry loads prior to washing. The board is detachable and the laundry bags are removable.

Below right: A wall-mounted ironing board unit lets you flip the board up and out of the way when not in use, concealed in a handsome wood cabinet. The cabinet has a shelf and outlet for the iron as well.

Ironing is generally not a favorite task, but if you use the right board and ironing-station organizer, the chore will be easier and more pleasant, and the board will never get in the way of the other things you have to do in the laundry room. Your choice of ironing board will basically come down to using a mounted board or a freestanding unit.

➤ MOUNTED IRONING BOARDS: A major advantage to wall-mounted boards is the access underneath. They let you iron difficult pieces such as dresses and pants more easily, by permitting the clothes to slide further onto the board without being impeded by board legs. There are two types of mounted boards: recessed and surface mounted. Recessed boards are completely hidden and out of the way when stored, while surface-mounted boards just fold up against the mounting platform in plain view.

Recessed (or hidden) ironing boards are a stylish option. The cabinet doors and interiors are available in many surface treatments

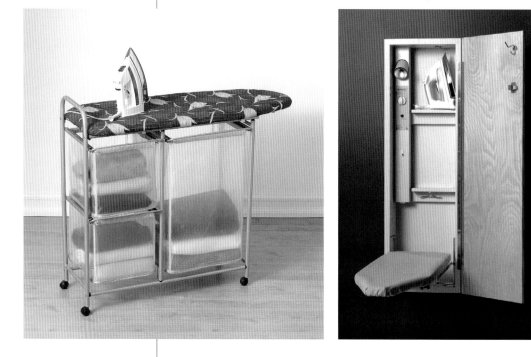

Keep ironing boards out of the way by using a wall hanger that stores the board flat against the wall and provides a shelf for the iron.

such as oak or pine. The recessed cabinet can be built to include storage for the iron and ironing supplies. But recessed boards require substantial modification of an existing wall. If you don't want to undertake such an extensive renovation, or if the laundry room doesn't have traditional walls, consider a surface-mounted board.

Surface-mounted ironing boards fold up and out of the way just as recessed boards do, but the surface-mounted version is more easily installed. The basic mounting plate and hinge unit can be attached to wall studs and masonry walls fairly simply. With this type of board, you'll need to create a separate place for the iron and ironing supplies. A shelf above the board unit is often the best solution.

➤ FREESTANDING IRONING BOARDS: These are the simplest and least expensive ironing boards. Most boards are adjustable for different heights, and you can select from different lengths. You can store your freestanding board on a hanging organizer that includes hooks for the board and a bin or shelf for the iron and supplies. This type of organizer is attached to the wall or hung from the side of a tall shelving unit or cabinet. If you don't have any wall space for your board, you can buy a board hanger that mounts on the back of a door or hangs from the top of the door.

ZONE 3

Drying and Folding Area

🕐 30 MINUTES

Folding clothes at a designated station in the laundry room is one way to diminish the possibility that clothes will become bedroom clutter. Unfolded clothes are too easily laid on a bed or chair to be folded later. It makes sense to include drying facilities in this zone because drying the clothes prepares them for folding or hanging.

➤ DRYING AIDS: There are many types of structures to efficiently dry clothes in the space you have available.

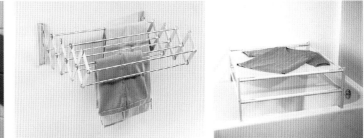

Left: Retractable clotheslines can be used indoors or out, mounting quickly and easily to a wall.

Center: A fold-out drying rack attaches to a wall or solid door, and collapses almost flat. Pulled out, the rack holds a small laundry load's worth of garments.

Right: A simple stackable dryer can be handy for drying delicates and sweaters. It can be placed over a sink or on a countertop—even on top of your dryer.

Drying racks come in all shapes and sizes, in wood and metal. Many are expandable, and some include flat drying shelves as well as the traditional bars for drying. If you dry mostly loose items such as stockings, socks, and undergarments, a basic rack may do the trick. If you tend to dry delicate blouses or sweaters, you'll probably need a rack with drying shelves. On metal drying racks, the bars should be coated or stainless steel to avoid staining delicate fabrics.

A drying line can be an excellent option in laundry rooms that are cramped for floor space, but with plenty of overhead space. You can use a regular clothesline running between hooks attached to two facing walls, or use the more upscale option of a "hotel-style" retractable drying line.

Fold-out hanging bars are attached to a wall or the back of a door for hang-drying loose garments or storing newly pressed shirts and clothes on hangers. These can be folded out of the way when not in use.

➤ FOLDING SPACE: Every laundry room benefits from a specific area for folding laundry. The task will go faster and your clean clothes will stay more organized when all the folding is done in one place. You don't necessarily need a lot of space, because you can only fold one garment at a time. A deep countertop is best, because it lets you completely lay

THE INSIDE SCOOP

POP AND DRY: Sweaters can be difficult garments to dry: they can't be hung or they will stretch, and the fabric is usually too delicate for tumble drying. Laying them flat on a towel can take a long time. But "pop-open" sweater dryers work fast and easily. Just pop the dryer open (it looks like a potato chip made out of window screen) and lay the sweater over the curve of the dryer. The shape of the dryer and its screened body allow for maximum air circulation and quick drying. When you're done, just fold the dryer up and store it on a shelf or in a cabinet.

BAG TIME: Mesh bags are wonderful for washing lingerie and other delicates, but they need a place to go when not in use. Hang the bags from hooks on the wall or under a cabinet or shelf positioned over the washing machine. This will ensure that they are within arm's reach when you're sorting clothes to go into the washing machine, and hanging them will let them dry after use.

out whatever you are folding. If your laundry room does not have a countertop, customize one. Create a folding surface out of a piece of plywood or sheet of hard plastic large enough to fit over the top surface of your dryer, or washer and dryer. Fold the clothes on top as you pull them out of the dryer. Or use a hinged countertop crafted from a piece of plywood and sturdy hinges attached to the wall. Keep hangers near the ironing board. Hang shirts and other permanent-press items on them as soon as they come out of the dryer so that you won't have to iron them. Use a wall- or door-mounted folding hanging rod or a hanging stand to keep shirts in order until you put them away.

ZONE 4

Soaking Area

15 MINUTES

Every laundry room should have a durable "slop sink" for soaking garments and hand-washing delicates such as sweaters. Hang a rag or paper-towel hanger within arm's reach of the sink so that you can clean up spills as soon as they occur. Keep a wire or plastic-mesh bin in the sink as a place to put garments to drain so you still have access to the sink.

KEEPING UP

Because life is so busy, the laundry area can easily fall into disarray. Here's how to make sure your laundry area stays clutter free.

• **Inventory analysis:** Before your weekly grocery-shopping trip, check the supplies-storage area of your laundry room. Return supplies that have been scattered about the room to their proper area, and check for supplies that need to be replenished.

• **Orphan patrol:** Once a week—not when you're doing laundry—visit the laundry room to check for leftover soaking, dried, or dirty clothes. Return these orphans to their correct locations.

Photography Credits

Photo by Grey Crawford, 9, 12

Photo by Beth Singer, kitchen design by Kris Atwood, Atwood: Fine Architectural Cabinetry, Birmingham, MI, 14–15

Photo courtesy of Plain & Fancy Custom Cabinetry, 16

Photo courtesy of Plain & Fancy Custom Cabinetry, 18

Photo courtesy of KraftMaid Cabinetry, 800/571-1990, www.kraftmaid.com, 19

Photo courtesy of KraftMaid Cabinetry, 800/571-1990, www.kraftmaid.com, 20

Photo courtesy of Rubbermaid, 888 895-2110, www.rubbermaid.com, 20

Photo courtesy of Wood-Mode Fine Custom Cabinetry, 877 635-7500, www.wood-mode.com, 21

Photo courtesy The Container Store, 800-786-7315, www.containerstore.com, 22

Photo courtesy of Plain & Fancy Custom Cabinetry, 23

Photo courtesy of Lillian Vernon, www.lillianvernon.com, 800 LILLIAN, 24

Photo courtesy The Container Store, 800-786-7315, www.containerstore.com, 25

Photo courtesy of Plain & Fancy Custom Cabinetry, 28

Photo courtesy of KraftMaid Cabinetry, 800/571-1990, www.kraftmaid.com, 29

Photo courtesy of KraftMaid Cabinetry, 800/571-1990, www.kraftmaid.com, 29

Photo courtesy of Wood-Mode Fine Custom Cabinetry, 877 635-7500, www.wood-mode.com, 30

Photo courtesy of Wood-Mode Fine Custom Cabinetry, 877 635-7500, www.wood-mode.com, 31

Photo courtesy The Container Store, 800-786-7315, www.containerstore.com, 32

Photo courtesy of Wood-Mode Fine Custom Cabinetry, 877 635-7500, www.wood-mode.com, 33

Photo courtesy of J.C. Penney, 34

Photo courtesy of Rubbermaid, 888 895-2110, www.rubbermaid.com, 35

©Photo Courtesy California Closets, 37

Photo courtesy of Wood-Mode Fine Custom Cabinetry, 877 635-7500, www.wood-mode.com, 38

Photo courtesy of Wood-Mode Fine Custom Cabinetry, 877 635-7500, www.wood-mode.com, 38

Photo by Snaidero Kitches + Design, www.snaidero-usa.com, 39

Photo courtesy of Grange Furniture, Inc, 1.800.GRANGE.1, www.grange.fr, 42

Photo courtesy of Rubbermaid, 888 895-2110, www.rubbermaid.com, 48

©Photo Courtesy California Closets, 49

Photo courtesy of Rubbermaid, 888 895-2110, www.rubbermaid.com, 50

©Photo Courtesy California Closets, 51

Photo courtesy of Lillian Vernon, www.lillianvernon.com, 800 LILLIAN, 51

Photo courtesy of Rubbermaid, 888 895-2110, www.rubbermaid.com, 52

Photo courtesy of Rubbermaid, 888 895-2110, www.rubbermaid.com, 53

Photo by Mick Hales, 55

Photo by Gridley & Graves, 56

Photo by Brad Simmons, 57

Photo courtesy of Lillian Vernon, www.lillianvernon.com, 800 LILLIAN, 58

Photo by Brad Simmons, 59

Photo by Gross & Daley, 60

©Photo Courtesy California Closets, 61

Photo courtesy of Lillian Vernon, www.lillianvernon.com, 800 LILLIAN, 62

Photo courtesy of Lillian Vernon, www.lillianvernon.com, 800 LILLIAN, 62

©Photo Courtesy California Closets, 63

©Photo Courtesy California Closets, 63

Photo courtesy of Rubbermaid, 888 895-2110, www.rubbermaid.com, 64

Photo courtesy of Rubbermaid, 888 895-2110, www.rubbermaid.com, 65

Photo courtesy of Grange Furniture, Inc, 1.800.GRANGE.1, www.grange.fr, 66

Photo courtesy of Grange Furniture, Inc, 1.800.GRANGE.1, www.grange.fr, 66

Photo courtesy of Ligne Roset, 67

Photo by Brad Simmons, 68

Photo by Brian Hagiwara, 71

©Photo Courtesy California Closets, 74

Photo courtesy of Lillian Vernon, www.lillianvernon.com, 800 LILLIAN, 75

Photo by Gross & Daley, 76

Photo courtesy of Rubbermaid, 888 895-2110, www.rubbermaid.com, 77

Photo courtesy of Lillian Vernon, www.lillianvernon.com, 800 LILLIAN, 77

Photo courtesy of Lillian Vernon, www.lillianvernon.com, 800 LILLIAN, 78

Photo courtesy of J.C. Penney, 79

Photo courtesy The Container Store, 800-786-7315, www.containerstore.com, 80

Photo courtesy The Container Store, 800-786-7315, www.containerstore.com, 81

Photo courtesy of Lillian Vernon, www.lillianvernon.com, 800 LILLIAN, 82

Photo courtesy of J.C. Penney, 82

Photo by Gross & Daley, 83

Photo courtesy of Rubbermaid, 888 895-2110, www.rubbermaid.com, 85

Photo courtesy The Container Store, 800-786-7315, www.containerstore.com, 86

Photo courtesy of Lillian Vernon, www.lillianvernon.com, 800 LILLIAN, 87

©Photo Courtesy California Closets, 88

Photo courtesy of Lillian Vernon, www.lillianvernon.com, 800 LILLIAN, 90

Photo courtesy of Lillian Vernon, www.lillianvernon.com, 800 LILLIAN, 90

Photo by Kaskel Architectural Photography, Inc, 92

Photo by Hotze Eisma, 94–95

Photo by Gross and Daley, 97

Photo courtesy of Rubbermaid, 888 895-2110, www.rubbermaid.com, 98

Photo courtesy of J.C. Penney, 98

Photo courtesy of Rubbermaid, 888 895-2110, www.rubbermaid.com, 101

Photo courtesy of Lillian Vernon, www.lillianvernon.com, 800 LILLIAN, 101

Photo by David Livingston, 102

Photo courtesy of Rubbermaid, 888 895-2110, www.rubbermaid.com, 103

Photo courtesy of Lillian Vernon, www.lillianvernon.com, 800 LILLIAN, 104

Photo courtesy of Lillian Vernon, www.lillianvernon.com, 800 LILLIAN, 105

Photo courtesy of Lillian Vernon, www.lillianvernon.com, 800 LILLIAN, 106

Photo courtesy of Rubbermaid, 888 895-2110, www.rubbermaid.com, 106

Photo courtesy of Lillian Vernon, www.lillianvernon.com, 800 LILLIAN, 106

Photo courtesy of Lillian Vernon, www.lillianvernon.com, 800 LILLIAN, 108

Photo courtesy of J.C. Penney, 108

Photo courtesy of Rubbermaid, 888 895-2110, www.rubbermaid.com, 109

Photo courtesy of J.C. Penney, 109

Photo courtesy of Rubbermaid, 888 895-2110, www.rubbermaid.com, 110

Photo by Dominique Vorillon, 112

Photography © 2003 by Edward Barr, 114–115

Photo by Gross & Daley, 116

Photo by Gross & Daley, 117

Photo courtesy of Sanus Systems, 800 359-5520, www.sanus.com, 118

Photo courtesy of Sanus Systems, 800 359-5520, www.sanus.com, 121

Photo courtesy of Sanus Systems, 800 359-5520, www.sanus.com, 122

Photo courtesy of Sanus Systems, 800 359-5520, www.sanus.com, 122

Photo courtesy of Lillian Vernon, Inc, 123

Photo by Brad Simmons, 124

Photo by Bill Holt, 125

Photo courtesy of Stacks and Stacks, 800-761-5222, www.stacksandstacks.com, 126

Photo by Gross & Daley, 127

Photo courtesy of J.C. Penney, 129

Photo by Gross & Daley, 133

Photo courtesy of Grange Furniture, Inc, 1.800.GRANGE.1, www.grange.fr, 136

Photo courtesy of Grange Furniture, Inc, 1.800.GRANGE.1, www.grange.fr, 139–138

Photo by Michael Luppino, 140

Photo courtesy of Grange Furniture, Inc, 1.800.GRANGE.1, www.grange.fr, 143

Photo by Mick Hales, 143

Photo courtesy of JC Penney, 144

Photo courtesy of Lillian Vernon, www.lillianvernon.com, 800 LILLIAN, 145

Photo courtesy of Lillian Vernon, www.lillianvernon.com, 800 LILLIAN, 145

Photo courtesy of Grange Furniture, Inc, 1.800.GRANGE.1, www.grange.fr, 146

Photo by Guy Bouchet, 147

Photo by Eric Roth, 148

Photo courtesy of J.C. Penney, 148

Photo courtesy of Rubbermaid, 888 895-2110, www.rubbermaid.com, 150

Photo courtesy of Rubbermaid, 888 895-2110, www.rubbermaid.com, 154

Photo courtesy of Rubbermaid, 888 895-2110, www.rubbermaid.com, 156

Photo courtesy of Rubbermaid, 888 895-2110, www.rubbermaid.com, 159

Photo courtesy of Rubbermaid, 888 895-2110, www.rubbermaid.com, 161

Photo courtesy of Rubbermaid, 888 895-2110, www.rubbermaid.com, 162

Photo courtesy of J.C. Penney, 163

Photo courtesy of Rubbermaid, 888 895-2110, www.rubbermaid.com, 163

Photo courtesy of Rubbermaid, 888 895-2110, www.rubbermaid.com, 164

©Photo Courtesy California Closets, 166

©Photo Courtesy California Closets, 168–169

Photo courtesy of StoreWall LLC, 866 889-2502, www.storewall.com, 170

Photo courtesy of Lillian Vernon, www.lillianvernon.com, 800 LILLIAN, 171

©Photo Courtesy California Closets, 173

Photo courtesy of Rubbermaid, 888 895-2110, www.rubbermaid.com, 174

Photo courtesy of Rubbermaid, 888 895-2110, www.rubbermaid.com, 175

Photo courtesy of JC Penney, 176

Photo courtesy of Rubbermaid, 888 895-2110, www.rubbermaid.com, 176

Photo courtesy of Rubbermaid, 888 895-2110, www.rubbermaid.com, 177

Photo courtesy of Rubbermaid, 888 895-2110, www.rubbermaid.com, 177

Photo courtesy of Rubbermaid, 888 895-2110, www.rubbermaid.com, 178

Photo courtesy of Rubbermaid, 888 895-2110, www.rubbermaid.com, 178

Photo courtesy of Rubbermaid, 888 895-2110, www.rubbermaid.com, 178

Photo courtesy of Rubbermaid, 888 895-2110, www.rubbermaid.com, 179

Photo courtesy of JC Penney, 180

Photo by Bruce Buck, 182

Photo courtesy of JC Penney, 184

©Photo Courtesy California Closets, 185

Photo courtesy of JC Penney, 187

Photo courtesy of Stacks and Stacks, 800-761-5222, www.stacksandstacks.com, 186

Photo courtesy of Rubbermaid, 888 895-2110, www.rubbermaid.com, 188

Photo courtesy of Lillian Vernon, www.lillianvernon.com, 800 LILLIAN, 189

Photo courtesy The Container Store, 800-786-7315, www.containerstore.com, 192

©Photo Courtesy California Closets, 191

©Photo Courtesy California Closets, 190

©Photo Courtesy California Closets, 194

©Photo Courtesy California Closets, 196–197

Photo courtesy of Plain & Fancy Custom Cabinetry, 199

©Photo Courtesy California Closets, 200

Photo courtesy of Rubbermaid, 888 895-2110, www.rubbermaid.com, 201

Photo courtesy of Lillian Vernon, www.lillianvernon.com, 800 LILLIAN, 201

©Photo Courtesy California Closets, 202

©Photo Courtesy California Closets, 203

Photo courtesy of JC Penney, 206

Photo courtesy of JC Penney, 205

Photo courtesy of JC Penney, 208

Photo courtesy The Container Store, 800-786-7315, www.containerstore.com, 209

©Photo Courtesy California Closets, 211

Photo courtesy of Rubbermaid, 888 895-2110, www.rubbermaid.com, 204

©Photo Courtesy California Closets, 212

Photo courtesy The Container Store, 800-786-7315, www.containerstore.com, 214

©Photo Courtesy California Closets, 216–217

Photo courtesy of Rubbermaid, 888 895-2110, www.rubbermaid.com, 218

©Photo Courtesy California Closets, 218

Photo courtesy of Rubbermaid, 888 895-2110, www.rubbermaid.com, 218

Photo courtesy of Iron-A-Way, 800-536-9495, www.ironaway.com, 220

Photo courtesy of Lillian Vernon, www.lillianvernon.com, 800 LILLIAN, 220

Photo courtesy of Lillian Vernon, www.lillianvernon.com, 800 LILLIAN, 222

Photo courtesy of Lillian Vernon, www.lillianvernon.com, 800 LILLIAN, 222

Photo courtesy of Lillian Vernon, www.lillianvernon.com, 800 LILLIAN, 222

Photo courtesy of Rubbermaid, 888 895-2110, www.rubbermaid.com, 221

Index